the sustainable asian house

PAUL McGILLICK

Photography by MASANO KAWANA

TUTTLE Publishing

Tokyo | Rutland, Vermont | Singapore

CONTENTS

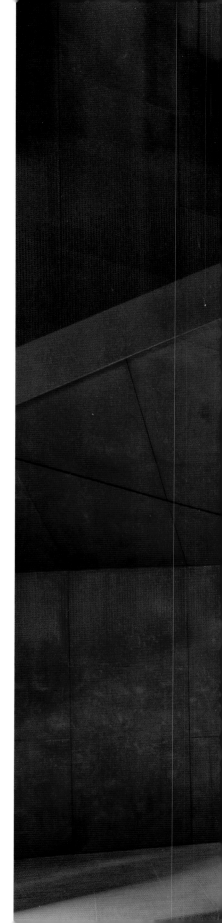

The Party House in Sentosa, Singapore (page 128), is a collection of coloured glass boxes designed to bring people together.

THE STORY OF SUSTAINABILITY

Much has been written over the last twenty years or so about how residential architecture in Southeast Asia has explored strategies for working with the tropical climate. Note my use of the word 'with', because we are not talking here of 'coping' with the climate or 'overcoming' the climate, but of developing ways of adapting to the climate in order to achieve a sustainable way of life. This agenda has been driven by a desire to live more authentically by engaging with the natural world, by health issues such as the need to avoid unnaturally cold air-conditioned environments and the thermal shock of moving in and out of air-conditioning, and, above all, by the need to conserve energy and avoid unnecessary damage to the global ecosystem. The rapid evolution of such climatic strategies has resulted in an approach which could be almost deemed a celebration of the climate, replacing the previous implied idea that the tropical climate was somehow our enemy.

This has been part of a broader agenda which has been as much political, economic and social as it has been environmental. The aim has been to find ways to live appropriately in the contemporary, tropical world. This, in turn, implies the need for local solutions rather than those imposed from elsewhere—a one size fits all solution which, in architectural language, invariably means International Modernism. Hence, terms like 'Tropical Modern' and 'Modern Regional' were used to pin down the emergence of architectural strategies which sought to adapt International Modernism to a tropical climate and to local cultures. In other words, there was an attempt to preserve the universally applicable and beneficial aspects of International Modernism while achieving an architecture appropriate for its place.

'… a return to living in a culturally and climatically authentic way.'

The debate surrounding this agenda has commonly been framed against a colonial background. The imposition of foreign rule was understood to imply the imposition of many other things, including building types. Hence, political and economic emancipation suggested a broader emancipation, a whole new way of life based on traditional values and free of imposed Western values, a return to living in a culturally and climatically authentic way.

Then along came globalization. Now the world was becoming increasingly integrated economically and commercially, and with it came a kind of 'mass

cult', yet another imposition of a uniform culture from elsewhere which had little regard for regional and cultural differences. Arguably, the new globalization was really only colonialism dressed up in new clothes, since the epicentres of the global economy, at least until the recent emergence of China and India as economic powerhouses, were still the former colonial capitals.

Colonialism can be viewed as an early form of globalization. It may have lacked the communications technology which now enables instantaneous communication throughout the world, the means of transport available may have been slower and more primitive, and the goods being traded may have been different, but the motivation was largely economic. While there were undoubtedly exceptions, it was usually a case of the flag following trade, with colonial rule evolving to protect the colonialists' economic interests.

Colonialism was, in fact, itself part of a broader phenomenon. It must be remembered that Thailand was never colonized. Nor was Japan. China, while it may have been commercially bullied by the West, with the exception of several foreign enclaves situated in seaports, continued to govern itself. Yet, these countries, as much as those that were colonized, engaged with an international economy, adopted many Western cultural mores and, especially in the capital cities and seaports, became increasingly 'Westernized'.

This introduction is not the place to expand any further on these issues. Nor do I wish to comprehensively discuss the recent evolution of the tropical Southeast Asian house. Robert Powell's books (the key ones are listed in the Select Bibliography at the end of this book) do this with far more authority than I can offer, as does Amanda Achmadi's fluent overviews of modern Indonesian architecture in *25 Tropical Houses in Indonesia* (2006) and *Houses for the 21st Century* (2004).

I mention these matters mainly to show that things are a lot more complex than is sometimes suggested, but also to establish a slightly different context in which to discuss the houses selected for this book.

WHAT THIS BOOK IS ABOUT

When you see the word 'sustainable' in the title you will assume that we are looking at houses which are sustainable in the sense that they minimize their impact on their immediate physical environment as well as minimize their use of non-renewable resources (energy and materials) in the building and running

The Carphenie House in Kuala Lumpur (page 42) brings green space inside its bold, circular entry void, which is open to the sky.

The 27 houses featured in the book have also been carefully selected to show how architecture is responding to changing demographics in Southeast Asian societies. With ever-accelerating urbanization as a result of both urban drift and natural population increase, and with new professions emerging all the time, there is a need for a wide range of accommodation in order to sustain changing lifestyles. For example, in contrast to their parents, a younger generation working in new professions may live by themselves or as childless couples and be keen to stay close to all the action associated with urban centres. The growing middle class is also producing smaller families, replacing the large families of the past and accordingly requiring different kinds of accommodation.

The point is that a home is the most crucial way in which we sustain ourselves. To be homeless is to live an unsustainable life. Not only do we all need a home, we all want one that will sustain us in our chosen way of life. But this sustainability is an integral part of an ecosystem. One aspect is how we live with the climate in a rational and responsible way. But it is just as important to put in place strategies which, for example, sustain the family, whether it be the nuclear family or the extended family, taking into account the differing needs of parents, children and grandparents, as well as their broader social needs. Often this is an issue of *reconciling privacy and community*. In the societies of Southeast Asia, community has traditionally taken precedence over privacy. However, with the super-charged growth of the technological global economy, demographics are changing and a new generation is demanding more privacy, but not necessarily at the cost of community. Hence, the question becomes: How do we design dwellings and their urban context so that the inhabitants can enjoy higher levels of privacy without losing that sense of familial and social community which has sustained tropical Asian communities in the past?

These are serious issues which contemporary architects are charged with addressing. But, at times in this book, I am also a little tongue in cheek. The Party House on Sentosa Island in Singapore may, for example, seem an unlikely inclusion in such a book, being a house devoted solely to having parties. But, apart from being a splendid piece of residential architecture, it does serve a genuinely sustainable purpose by sustaining social relations, and it does so in a remarkably imaginative way.

of those houses—with the implication that they do so in a way that still enables a comfortable way of life and provides for the needs of a diverse range of inhabitants. You are right in this assumption. But the scope of the book is greater than that.

'… in this book I look at houses not just from the environmentally sustainable point of view, but also from the personal, social and cultural points of view.'

What we now call sustainability we used to call ecology. 'Ecology' may have been rather inexact, but it was very useful as a term because it drew attention to the world as an ecology, that is, a system in which all the constituent parts exist in relation to one another, and where any change to one part of the system will affect all the other parts.

Therefore, in this book I look at houses not just from the environmentally sustainable point of view, but also from the personal, social and cultural points of view. Hence, there are houses which are interesting mainly because of the environmental strategies employed. But there are others which are interesting for the ways in which, say, they sustain the extended family in the context of the 'global village'. Or they may aim to sustain cultural traditions, including crafts, which are increasingly under threat.

SUSTAINABLE LIVING IN THE TROPICS

The current preoccupation with environmentally sustainable domestic architecture in the tropics could lead us to overlook the fact that this has been going on for a long time, probably as long as human beings have lived in tropical climates. Vernacular architecture has long employed a variety of strategies to cope with a hot, humid climate. While different regions throughout Southeast Asia may have developed different characteristics, they also have a lot in common. High pitched roofs, wide eaves, air vents, timber shutters or blinds, courtyards, elevation off the ground and tiled flooring are some typical climate control strategies used in different ways throughout the region.

Vernacular forms evolved usually in response to demographic shifts, including immigration and colonization. The shophouse is a good example. It is found throughout the region, from Thailand to Indonesia, in a variety of forms. Initially an imported phenomenon, it has been in Southeast Asia long enough to have become part of the urban vernacular. Its commercial function helped its environmental agenda. By locating the business at the front and domestic living in the centre and back of the building, a buffer from the sun was automatically provided for the inhabitants. Commonly, an internal courtyard and air-well provided further protection as well as generating air circulation. After losing many shophouses to demolition in the post-war development push, they are now often protected, and certainly sought after for their urban location and their potential for reinvention. The reworked shophouse is sustainable on a number of levels: it avoids demolition and rebuilding, it offers an existing programme of climate abatement, and it is a way of sustaining cultural heritage. At the same time, it exudes character. Sensitively handled, the reinvented shophouse provides a distinctive private home for contemporary living.

'... contemporary climate-responsive Southeast Asian architecture is part of an ongoing evolution....'

The bungalow (from the Hindustani word *bangala*) is another imported form, brought to the Straits Settlements by British colonialists and evolving in a variety of ways, including the black-and-white house. Julian Davison lists their climate abatement strategies: the timber and *atap* (thatch) upper storey absorbed heat slowly and protected the masonry ground floor, often tiled, from the heat; there was further protection from overhangs and blinds; a high roof profile created a chimney effect to draw hot air up and out through vents; it was raised on brick piers with ground floor air vents to generate air circulation. Davison concludes that 'the black-and-white house was well-adapted to Singapore's equatorial monsoon climate, turning what might have been simply a stylistic exercise—a local parody of the Tudorbethan revival back in England—into a domestic architecture that was at once charming and also well suited to the environment' (2006: 3).

Arguably, the post-war period throughout the region saw a retreat from climatically responsive architecture in favour of an imposed, compromised and reductionist version of modernism until the vernacular revival of the 1970s and 1980s saw a revisiting of traditional climate strategies.

The point is that contemporary climate-responsive Southeast Asian architecture is part of an ongoing evolution, a constant conversation, and a continuing 'negotiation between foreign architectural ideas and the local context which includes lifestyle and culture, the tropical climate and traditional architectural vocabularies' (Duangrit Bunnag, 2003: 10).

HOUSE AND HOME

Let's look now at the notion of sustainability from a slightly different perspective—from that of the home.

A house is not necessarily a home. A look at the kinds of metaphors we use is a clue to that. We talk about 'housing' something, meaning to put something into a container, but without any implication as to the quality of that container. But when we talk about feeling 'at home', there is a clear sense that we are now in a place where we feel comfortable, a place which is right for us.

A house is a shelter, offering protection. But a home is much more than simply a physical shelter. It *sustains* us emotionally, spiritually and culturally. The question therefore arises: In what ways does a house do this and to what extent can the design of the house assist?

'... architecture can certainly facilitate that feeling of being at home.'

The great Dutch architect and urbanist Aldo van Eyck once remarked that 'architecture must facilitate man's homecoming'. A beautiful house is no

The master bedroom in Sacha Cotture's home in Manila (page 168) is set back from the front façade and screened by treated bamboo.

guarantee that it will also be a home. Equally, a house that is poorly designed does not necessarily prevent it from being a true home for its inhabitants. But the architecture of the structure can certainly facilitate that feeling of being at home.

What, then, makes a house a home? This requires that we look at the various functions of a home.

Frank Lloyd Wright famously said that a home needed to offer refuge and prospect. Let's consider refuge first. At one time, the home was considered a refuge from potentially threatening interlopers. Indeed, this is still the case, and throughout Southeast Asia there is a heightened sense of threat from intruders which has led architects to design houses which frequently turn their back on the street, both as a defensive posture and as a tactic not to reveal what may be attractive to thieves. But this, at least, has the virtue of creating some exciting arrival sequences.

But the home today is also a refuge from an increasingly noisy, busy and intrusive world. It is a place to retreat to, an escape from the hectic everyday world outside. For some of the houses in this book, location alone helps to provide this refuge. For others, the planning provides insulation from the hyperactivity just outside the front door.

But hiding away in a box is neither pleasant nor healthy. Human beings need to be connected with the world, both physically and emotionally, whether it be the macro world outside or the micro world they create for themselves inside. Hence, the need for prospect—to look out on to something bigger, more airy, and especially to connect with the natural word. Again, there are houses in this book which are privileged by their location and enjoy such wonderful prospect out to a natural world, including their own gardens, that they are effectively a part of that landscape. Others need to borrow landscape, with architects adopting the traditional Japanese aesthetic of carefully framing views to the outside to create the illusion of being a part of a landscape without intrusion from the neighbouring non-natural world. This is nowhere more urgent than in an apartment, and the Brookvale Apartment in Singapore (page 74), the only apartment included in this book, is a perfect example.

Turning one's back on an urban environment may mean creating one's own internal landscape. Hence, the prospect may be out to an internal garden courtyard. Equally, it may involve internal prospect where the interior of the house itself becomes a landscape and any sense of containment is ameliorated by views across and through different interior spaces. This is a crucial element of the modernist approach which has been absorbed into the Asian house, namely, a plan of free-flowing spaces where the spaces are functionally distinguished only by partial or very subtle separation. If Asian models have been modified by this International Modernist strategy, the strategy itself is often modified by another adaptation from Japan, namely, an internal prospect which has glimpses of external prospect in the form of small or slot windows on to miniature garden courtyards, and sometimes not so miniature, or even external, courtyards as with the Carphenie House on the outskirts of Kuala Lumpur (page 42).

External prospect, however, is increasingly becoming more than simply visual connection. More and more often, the connection is literally physical, with the house connected directly to the outside landscape. This serves an environmental purpose, of course, because verandahs, extended overhangs, free-flowing interior spaces and breezeways generate cross-ventilation. But the separation of inside and outside is also becoming blurred. More and more frequently, the house embraces the outside landscape as an essential part of healthy living, both in the physical and in the emotional sense. Living *with* the tropical climate has been extended to celebrating and enjoying the tropical landscape rather than keeping it at arm's length.

Arguably, International Modernism had its origins not with the usual suspects like Le Corbusier, Mies van der Rohe and the Bauhaus, but with the Arts and Crafts Movement which flourished through the second half of the nineteenth century and into the 1930s and was exported from Britain to Europe and Asia—which would support my argument here that current sustainable practices in Southeast Asian houses are part of an ongoing evolution and an aspect of a continuing conversation between differing traditions. The black-and-white houses in Singapore and their Malaysian variants are obvious examples where there was a meeting of the Indian bungalow, local vernacular forms and Arts and Crafts influences. The black-and-white houses are now heritage-protected and are commonly subject to highly sensitive retrofitting and restoration for contemporary living. Moreover, their sustainable features, such as free-flowing spaces, wide verandahs, extended eaves, cross-ventilation and air vents, are being adopted in many newly built houses.

'The importance of well-being is reflected in the emphasis on fresh air, natural light and spatial variety to accommodate individual needs.'

Significantly, the Arts and Crafts Movement emphasized issues which perfectly encapsulate the strategies of the contemporary sustainable Asian house. For example, new architectural approaches involve the reinterpretation of vernacular practices with a growing interest in sustaining traditional crafts. Materials and construction techniques are taken from the local context. A degree of stylistic eclecticism is prominent. The importance of well-being is reflected in the emphasis on fresh air, natural light and spatial variety to accommodate individual needs. Designs also respond to climatic issues, such as orientation to the sun and prevailing winds.

This seems to be endorsed by Indian architect Rahul Mehrotra, who, when he speaks about the New Indian Modern could be describing the entire region. Mehrotra notes that New Indian Modern has 'evolved beyond its modernist roots to respond to the locale', but in so doing recognizes a key aspect of modernism which is invariably overlooked, namely, its core strategy of renewing the tradition through critical reflection. Mehrotra says that these architects 'recognize that modernism demands a respect for the inherent qualities of building materials, expressiveness of structure, the functional justification for form and the subtle integration of the icons and texture of the larger landscape in which they are set' (2011: 97).

SOCIAL SUSTAINABILITY

In the previous section I looked at what made a home and discussed the idea of how emotional and spiritual sustainability was implicit in the idea of home. Now we need to develop these ideas a little more and see how they inform the selection of the houses presented in this book.

Social sustainability is an issue both within the family and within the wider community. How, for example, does the home sustain the needs of families? How, also, does the home sustain healthy relationships between members of a family? And how does a house interact with its social context to sustain healthy social relationships?

In any society there is a constant negotiation between *community and privacy*. In Asian societies, in particular, it is probably true to say that, traditionally, community has taken precedence over privacy. The common good has always been promoted over individual needs or desires.

But all this is changing. Rapid urbanization, especially of the main cities, surging economic development, the emergence of an IT culture, global financial management, and globalization in general have instigated significant social change throughout Asia. New economic sectors have had an enormous impact on rising levels of education which, as a result, have spawned new professions. These factors have created new demographics, with priorities potentially at odds with traditional society.

The traditional extended family has been complemented by the emergence of the nuclear family: people who remain single by choice or otherwise, couples who have delayed having children, or couples with only one or two children. At the same time, a changing cultural landscape has seen a growing interest in urban engagement, although this is offset to some extent by growing anxiety about real or perceived threats to domestic security, leading to gated and guarded communities or other defensive strategies to protect the home.

'The extended family continues to sustain itself, but within an ongoing negotiation of greater privacy and independence for individuals within the family.'

These changes in the dynamics of traditional Asian families do not mean that newly urbanized Asia wants to throw out traditional values. What is

happening in reality is another version of the conversation-cum-negotiation I have already referred to—and further confirmation that architectural moves do not happen in isolation but as part of a wider context of social and political debate as well as economic diversification.

The extended family thus continues to sustain itself, but within an ongoing negotiation of greater privacy and independence for individuals within the family. There are a number of architectural models for this. On the one hand, there is the single dwelling planned to provide privacy for individuals but pivoting around communal spaces. Then there is a model which breaks this down to a greater or lesser extent by 'pavilionizing' the house. This may involve a series of linked pavilions or a family compound with independent pavilions, or even houses clustered around a central, shared court. Another variation is simply to purchase multiple adjacent lots or subdivide one large lot to enable adult children to live next door to their parents and/or siblings.

Within the nuclear family there is, as I noted earlier, a growing respect for the autonomy of children and their particular needs. As long ago as 1938, in *The Culture of Cities*, Lewis Mumford wrote that 'the child is no less entitled to space than the adult: he must have shelves and cupboards for his toys, room for play and movement, a place for quiet retreat and study, other than his bed. No housing standard is adequate that provides only cubicles or dressing rooms for the child, or forces him into the constant company of adults.' For the family to be truly sustainable, it is crucial to acknowledge that the world of the child is, despite its dependence on adults, a self-contained world with its own priorities and values. Equally, of course, parents are entitled to their own privacy and autonomy. These issues are addressed in house plans which clearly separate parent and children domains, again with linking communal areas where the family can come together.

The Ekamai house in Bangkok (page 28) illustrates a number of these issues in the one house. The free-flowing L-shaped plan of the ground floor offers direct connection to the garden court and a separate retreat for the couple's child, while upstairs adult and child domains are at either end connected by a perimeter corridor. At the same time, operable timber shutters connect the garden court with the life of the street outside. In this way, the house contributes to sustaining the character of the precinct without compromising its own privacy and security.

GATED AND GUARDED COMMUNITIES

As a number of the houses in this book are located in gated or guarded communities, we need to look briefly at how this increasingly prevalent phenomenon impacts on social sustainability. The separation of the guarded community from the wider community is delineated but does not involve a physical barrier, merely a security presence. Hence, it remains to some degree a part of the public domain. The gated community, however, is walled off and only authorized entry is permitted, making it private and exclusive.

It is often argued that the phenomenon is inimical to social sustainability. Given that the term includes the word 'community', we need to ask whether such developments really create a community or whether they are simply aggregations of dwellings whose long-term consequence is, in fact, alienation—alienation from the wider community, but also alienation for the people living in the gated/guarded communities because of the isolation which results from living in what is basically a suburb without any of the ebb and flow of human activity that typifies an organic community.

Whether gated or guarded, there is inevitably a loss of connection to the broader social world. The standard explanation for gated/guarded communities is fear. The inhabitants are seeking security from a perceived threat of assault and robbery. In some places this may be a very real threat. However, in a place

This house by Aamer Taher in Sentosa, Singapore
(page 114), is angled to maximize natural light.

like Singapore the threat is surely minimal. This suggests another motivation
for building in a gated/guarded community—status. Research supports this
contention, suggesting that 'exclusivity' has the double meaning of keeping
people out but also signalling social superiority. The reality is, however, that in
many places in Asia security is a real concern. In Jakarta, for example, memories
of the 1998 riots remain fresh. Moreover, there, as in Kuala Lumpur and Manila,
the threat of crime is quite palpable.

Every gated community is different from every other one. In many there
really is a community, one not just defined by a perimeter wall but by shared
values. This might be because the community represents a concentration of
people from the same religious community or, as in the case of the R House
in Tana Peru at Depok outside Jakarta (page 148), there is a concentration
of people with university ties. Often it will be the planning of the gated
community which helps generate a sense of community where no natural
affinities exist, as at the Kubik House in Ipoh, Malaysia (page 50), or at Tanah
Teduh in Jakarta (page 160).

A final caveat is the fact that many gated communities are actually quite
porous, as are guarded communities, with a constant flow of people and
transactions during the day and with full security applied only at night. Space
does not allow a fuller discussion of the issue. Suffice it to say that guarded
and gated communities come in many different forms and respond to many
different imperatives. Depending on how we look at them, and on how they
are planned, they can be either sustainable or unsustainable.

CULTURAL SUSTAINABILITY

Without identity, life is simply not sustainable at either the individual or the
community level. But identity is a social construct which can only be sustained
by continuing connection with a cultural tradition and by constant interrogation
in response to external change. The family home is an expression of the
identity of those who live in it. It does not exist in isolation, any more than
architecture operates in a social vacuum. Notwithstanding globalization, the
traditional societies of Southeast Asia are not about to abandon their cultural
heritage. But engagement with the global community requires an ongoing
negotiation if those communities are not to have their cultural identity
compromised.

*'An architecture of place is as much about cultural space as it is
physical space.'*

Exploring how to live with the climate in a responsible way is an opportunity
for the tropical societies of Southeast Asia to refine the contemporary dialectic
of identity. An architecture of place is as much about cultural space as it is
physical space. The two are, of course, inseparable, a fact highlighted by the
many homes, from Bali to Manila, which by virtue of an adopted international
style, inescapably reek of inauthenticity. These homes do not belong anywhere
unless it is in some fashionable, designosphere.

Abidin Kusno speaks of how young architects, through the Arsitek Muda
Indonesia in the 1990s, 'were more interested in "exploring design"
(*penjelajahan desain*) which they understood as a way of liberating their
individual creativity from the hegemony of functionalism and nationalism'
(2011: 87). This liberation is mirrored throughout the region and has meant
that architects could reexamine and reinvent traditional practice unclouded
by sentimental nationalism or a debased functionalism. It has resulted in an
architecture of place which typically uses, where possible, local materials, local
craftsmen and local crafts adapted to contemporary use.

The 27 houses in this book reveal a variety of approaches to cultural
sustainability. This may be illustrated in the way in which a house interacts
with its immediate urban context, or in the way the plan of a house reflects
traditional practice. It may be in the way traditional crafts are adapted to new
uses, or in the way local materials are used. It may also be in the way interior
details provide a sense of continuity in cultural and religious values across
generations.

If there is one defining characteristic of culturally sustainable architecture
in the region, it is its emphasis on materiality which implies an architecture
rooted in the everyday reality of its clients and where they live.

THAILAND

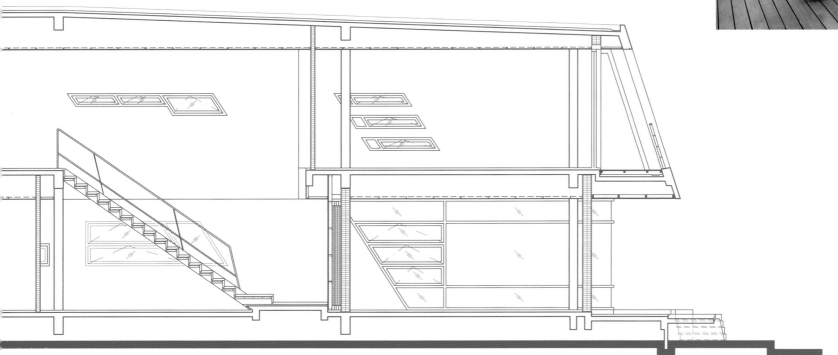

PRACHACHUEN HOUSE
BANGKOK, THAILAND
KANOON STUDIO

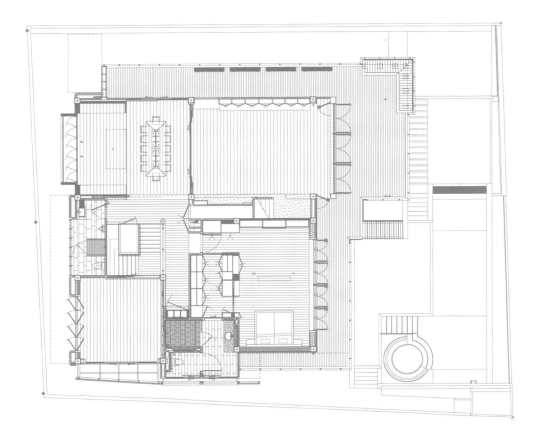

'We tried to make this house reflect the life of the client. The way we worked was that I let him tell me all his requirements. It was very much a process of give and take, compromises.'—Chartchalerm Klieopatinon

The architects at Kanoon Studio had worked with this client before so they knew he would continue to add to his long list of requirements. But they also knew that he was well informed about architecture and that he liked to work in a collaborative way.

There was no preconceived idea of what the house would look when it was finished. The plan was that it would grow with the design process—and after the house was finished—because the design allows for changes. It has a lot of inbuilt flexibility, which the architects refer to as 'latency'. By this, they mean they have provided everything the client wants but that extras are hidden. 'If he wants to separate a room', says Chartchalerm, 'he can do so. If he wants to expand his house, he can do that too. We tried to make the space quite open.'

The house is occupied by an extended family. The client's parents live with him, his brother lives next door (as part of the same plot) and the sons' rooms on the third floor are designed to be self-contained so that one of them can continue to live at home after marriage. The family comes from northern Thailand, which has a strong timber craft tradition, shared by the family. As a result, the house makes good use of recycled timber. The original idea was to renovate the existing house which the client had lived in for thirty years, but it was quickly apparent

that it would not accommodate the client's need for extra space, especially for entertaining. The original timber house was therefore demolished and the timber used for the front fence. In fact, the house makes extensive use of recycled timber—for the flooring, the ceilings, the interior panelling, the dining table top, some door frames and the entertainment deck.

The client's long experience of living on the site proved valuable when it came to how the site would be oriented. He knew the direction the wind came from, and since he was keen to maximize the use of natural ventilation this led to the idea of a wind chimney. In turn, this led to the idea of a rooftop entertainment area (with the potential for increased accommodation later) with a 'safari

Above The second level plan shows how the stairway and lift act as a pivot for the mainly public spaces.

Right The front fence is made of timber recycled from the original house that stood on the site.

roof' to capture the wind and draw it down, using the linking stairwell as a wind chimney to ventilate the house.

Initially, the client wanted the house to remain close to the garden, but the architects argued that they could push the natural ventilation agenda further if they lifted the house off the ground. The client agreed and now the deck is a viewing platform down to the pool and into the lush garden

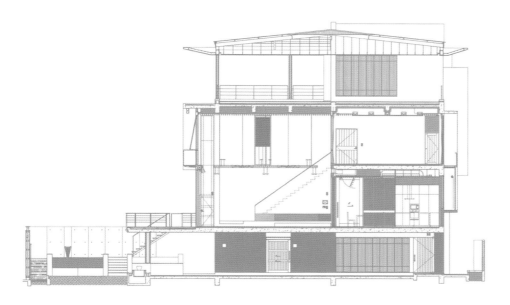

with its established Indian banyan tree and two frangipanis. These provide shade for the pool and both shade and privacy for the master bedroom.

The ground floor is reserved for parking, a laundry and wet kitchen, and ample storage, for example, a generous shoe storage room and wine cellar, and for partying around the pool. It is also the starting point for the quaint industrial-style lift with its antique carved wooden stool.

Level 2 is essentially a free-flowing space pivoting around the stairway. It contains a guest bathroom with a laminated, corrugated glass wall and benchtop made from recycled teak, a gym, the parents' room, an open-plan dry kitchen, a dining area and a double-height living area. The space can be opened up to the timber deck through fine steel-framed security doors off the kitchen and large sliding glass doors off the living area.

The spacious living area, with its contrasting facing walls, is the hub of the house. One wall is fully timber-panelled to conceal generous storage and is topped by clerestory windows, the other (by the stairwell to level 3) is a rendered wall with a Buddha shrine near the top, which doubles as a window from the master bedroom.

Level 3 houses the master bedroom and a music room for live performances. The music room has folding glass doors which open out on to the living space, effectively making the room a stage for performances. Heavy, carved traditional doors from India help isolate the room acoustically, while a bell and a red flashing light notify the musicians that there is somebody at the front door. The lady of the house has added a folding door to separate the master bedroom from the noise emanating from the music room!

This is a house that sustains an extended family and, through the use of recycled timber, their ties to their northern Thai origins. The inclusion of a wind chimney and the way the houses opens on to the shaded garden, means that the use of air-conditioning is reduced to the minimum. A highly flexible house, it manages to balance the occupants' enthusiasm for entertaining with their individual needs for privacy.

Left The double-height void of the living room provides a 'stage' for the music room.

Above This cross-section shows how the house is a vertical assemblage of spaces.

Below In the living room, joinery above the television provides storage space.

Far left The vestibule at the top of the stairs on the second level.

Left Floor-to-ceiling fenestration draws in natural light, while the rich vegetation outside provides sunscreening and privacy.

Right The barbeque area on the rooftop deck, which has the potential for further development.

Above The safari roof with its extended eaves.

Left The double-height living area with the Buddha shrine/window at top right.

Right The pool area enjoys ample shade from the well-established trees.

EQUILIBRIUM HOUSE
BANGKOK, THAILAND
VASLAB ARCHITECTURE

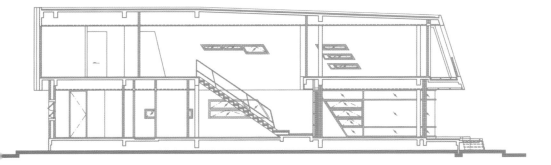

Left Long section.

Right The house consists of a number of refined concrete blocks and planes pulling in different directions but held together in equilibrium.

Below right The mix of chevron-shaped solids and voids gives the house a dynamic, futuristic quality.

'I like metaphor. I like meaning. I like the source of the origin and the outcome. There is a vocabulary of equilibrium throughout the house.'—Vasu Virajsilp

Sustaining the extended family in Asia has become a challenge in the new global economy, especially in the face of rapidly changing communications technology which threatens the survival of regional cultures. A younger generation of professionals has emerged who want greater independence and privacy but without necessarily losing the sense of community and continuity that the family unit provides.

As an alternative to accommodating the extended family in one building, some people have opted for family compounds, others for a variant whereby the parents buy an adjacent block of land for their children who then build their own house on it. This provides both community and privacy, with the additional benefit of added security, because each house can provide surveillance for the other. The Equilibrium House is an example of the latter solution to maintaining the extended family—connection with separation.

The client is an economics professor at a local university who lives in the house with his wife. He and the architect, Vasu Virajsilp, share the same aesthetic predisposition for clean, geometric lines and a fondness for concrete. Not surprisingly, they are both fans of Le Corbusier and Mies van der Rohe. The client requested a modern, low-maintenance home with a sense of pure form. He wanted it to have a 'masculine' or robust look and also that it be protective but not closed. He specified that the house be built in concrete with minimal use of other materials.

All of this suited Vasu. But, as he points out, this is not a public building but a home. He encouraged the client to use natural materials, especially timber, to complement as well as 'soften' the concrete, and to incorporate lots of visual connection to the garden and water court facing his parents' house next door and a 'green fence' to screen the living room from the road. The architect has also made a virtue out of the problem of getting a good concrete finish from Thai contractors by coating the concrete to 2–3 mm thickness. The look is smoother, the concrete is stronger and more durable, and maintenance is easier. The concrete also ends up with a variable tone so that it takes on a warmer and more decorative appearance. These strategies, says Vasu, make the house more liveable. Without them, it would be 'unsustainable'.

The hallmark of the building is a chevron form, a dynamic futuristic shape which animates the building inside and out. The thrusting diagonals maintain constant visual stimulation. They are forces which seem to be continually pulling away from one another. This is first seen in the external massing of the building, with the cantilevered box of the master bedroom thrusting out towards the street and apparently against the rest of the building. The angled garage columns, which in fact conceal a drainpipe, seem to push against the roof.

Inside the house, the chevron shape is repeated throughout, but each time in a slightly different way. For example, there are variations between the three chevron-shaped windows in the master bedroom, the windows in the dining room, the detailing in the stairwell, the staircase itself, and the shaped opening on the upper landing looking down into the dining room. The chevron shape creates a rhythm throughout the house and acts as a unifying element. All these opposing forces are kept in a permanent moment of equilibrium—hence the name of the house. According to Vasu, equilibrium is also a characteristic of his client who, as an economist, likes to maintain a state of order and balance.

The house is entered through the garden courtyard and then by way of a slightly elevated transitional terrace. The living, dining and pantry areas, together with a breakfast bench, comprise one continuous space. Sliding glass doors can close off the living room if desired. Teak is used for the flooring throughout and for the stairs. Above the dining space is an open well with a gallery linking the master bedroom at the front of the house with two other bedrooms at the rear.

The house does not set out to be a 'tropical' house. It is a highly transparent house, however, which aims to maintain a direct connection with the green exterior. It has a high degree of natural ventilation, sometimes in quite subtle ways, such as the air vents beneath the window facing the dining room and the translucent glass master bathroom with its partly open-to-the-sky dry pebble garden.

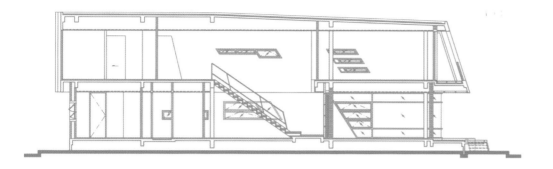

Left Floor-level air vents provide natural ventilation in the dining room area.

Below left A 'green fence' provides the necessary privacy to the fully transparent living room.

Above This section shows the void that effectively separates the house into two pavilions.

Right A view from the upper level down into the living/dining room void.

Below The dining area seen from the living room with the gallery void above it.

Above left and right Chevron shapes add a decorative touch to the master bedroom.

Left Running alongside the water feature, timber complements the finished concrete and glass.

Below The master bathroom with a view through to the outdoor pebble garden.

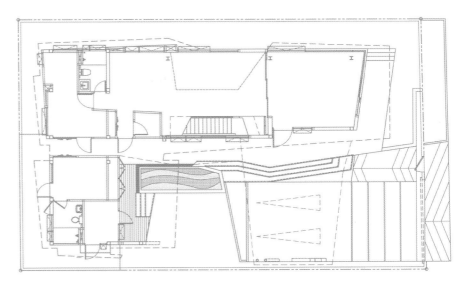

Right Ground floor plan.

Below The geometric complexity, viewed from the upper terrace, has a strong sculptural quality.

EKAMAI HOUSE
BANGKOK, THAILAND
CHAT ARCHITECTS

'I didn't want a big house and I didn't have a big budget. But when I was living in Thailand as a kid I loved the street culture. You had ice cream carts, junk men, dogs in the street, buffaloes. It's a sad scene now because there's no street culture any more.'—Chatpong Chuenrudeemol

Designing their own homes gives architects the opportunity to play with ideas and explore their own preoccupations. These days, clients typically want a house which turns its back on the street because security has become such a big issue. Architect Chatpong Chuenrudeemol understands this 'defensive mindedness', but he loves street life. When it came to designing his own home in the Ekamai district of Bangkok, he wanted to be able to balance his privacy and the need for security with engaging with the neighbourhood.

This interest in engagement is not just a sentimental idea. It is a recognition that social and cultural sustainability is as important as environmental sustainability. A large part of who we are is bound up with our cultural inheritance. Allowing a culture to die or cutting people off from a living tradition can lead to alienation, which is destructive at both the personal and social levels.

'For us', says Chatpong, 'it is important to find our own language that's rooted in culture, in the climate and in a lot of intangibles. And what I also think is important is the playfulness of Thai culture.'

Chatpong chose his site carefully. It is a corner block on a no-through road. There is, he says, a patchwork or quiltwork character to Bangkok's streets which he thinks this street typifies. The scale of the houses and the way they relate to the street

and to each other makes for what he calls a 'street room'. For this reason, he wanted to keep his house to the scale of its neighbours. Rather than have high ceilings on the ground level, he chose relatively low ceilings—'because I have a child and I wanted the ceilings at the scale of a child'—which gave him the flexibility to go higher on the upper level and maximize the use of natural light.

Above The internal courtyard looks towards his son's playroom.
Opposite above The house aims to engage with the street life of the neighbourhood.
Opposite below The shutters, made from a mix of recycled timbers, can be closed for privacy but also opened to engage with the street.

The plot is rectangular but the house is L-shaped, with the entry and garage at the foot of the long leg. Arrival is through the internal courtyard, which is formed by the L shape of the house and the long street elevation. The outer 'wall' of the house comprises a row of vertical timber shutters. As Chatpong explains, the wall 'redefines the perimeter wall urban house in Bangkok', which typically has a wall and the house set back from the wall, creating an unusable 'no-man's land' in between. During the day, the shutters open the courtyard to the street and draw air in to ventilate both the courtyard and the house. At night, or when the occupants are elsewhere, the house is secured by closing the shutters.

Just as the courtyard opens to the street, so the house also opens on to the courtyard. The north-facing aspect, along with a mature tree that serves as their 'canopy', ensures that the house is never subject to direct sunlight. In fact, the room most exposed is the upstairs western-facing bedroom

Below The timber shutters at street level are referenced on the upper level by the enfilade of timber-framed windows.

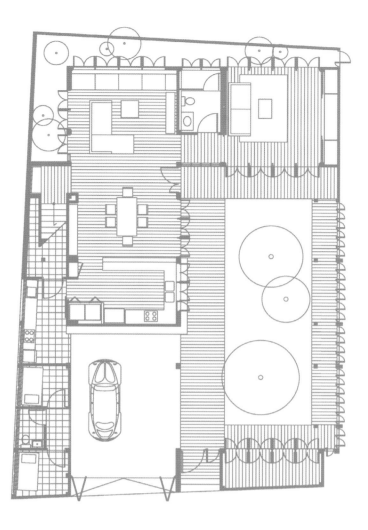

Left Ground floor plan.

Below left Looking from the son's playroom, the setback of the verandah and the tree ensure ample shading.

of Chat's son. But this borrows the lush garden of the next door neighbour to make it the coolest room in the house.

The courtyard and many features inside the house, such as the vertical casement windows upstairs and the narrow, vertical double doors downstairs, hint at traditional Thai houses with their typical use of timber, shutters and elongated proportions.

All of the timber used in the house is recycled from old Thai timber stilt houses. As Chat points out, using old timber is not only sustainable but also highly functional because it has been thoroughly cured and, therefore, is not susceptible to shrinkage. Door and window frames are all made from a local redwood hardwood. The louvres on the street wall are a mixed of recycled timbers, which give the shutters tonal variety. The floors and ceilings are made from *tabaag*, 'the poor man's teakwood', a wood that is commonly shunned. But it is a highly sustainable timber because it is fast growing and not endangered. It is also inexpensive and completely termite-resistant. It also provided Chat with a light-coloured local hardwood which is hard to source locally.

Otherwise, the house is made from plaster and concrete with great attention paid to fine detailing, for example, with the door and window frames and with the ledges and overhangs which protect the house from run-off staining.

The house is open plan with all spaces visually connected to one another. The downstairs is kitchen, dining and living, with a bathroom and Chat's son's 'everything room' on the short leg of the L, which also opens directly on to the courtyard. This room, which is self-contained and semi-independent of the rest of the house, is significant because it signals

Above When the shutters are open, the porosity of the house to the street is clear.

Above centre The son's playroom, located on the short end of the L-shaped house, overlooks the courtyard.

Right Blackboard-style sliding doors in the playroom hide books and toys and can also be drawn on.

a very specific understanding of the role of the child and his personal needs in the household. It is a recognition that the child is autonomous and not simply an extension of the parents. Hence, the child is given his own private space with its own entry.

With the aim of optimizing space, the stairway to the upper level uses the depth of the wall to form a bookcase. The upstairs of the house is also very open, with a corridor spine overlooking the courtyard and incorporating a storage banquette linking the two bedrooms with a sitting room and a bathroom in the middle.

True to the sustainable agenda of the house, Chat has preferred to use recycled furniture. Some of this is classic Scandinavian, but other pieces are

inherited, including his grandmother's sofa and his own childhood bed, now used by his son.

Affordable and sustainable in so many ways, the Ekamai House also exhibits a high level of contemporary refinement. At the same time, its contemporary character does not prevent it from being a 'good neighbour' and helping to sustain a sense of community.

Above The double-glass doors hint at traditional Thai houses.

Left The furnishings and the vertical casement windows in the living room contribute to a sense of cultural continuity.

Below The inset bookcase on the stairway maximizes available space.

THAILAND BANGKOK HOUSE   35

BANGKOK HOUSE
BANGKOK, THAILAND
SCOTT WHITTAKER

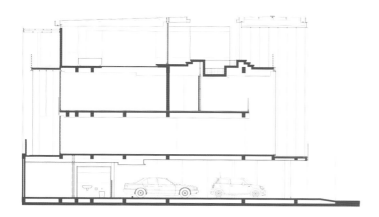

Scott Whittaker is an Australian architect who initially came to Bangkok on a two-year contract but has been living there now for 22 years, in the process establishing the highly successful international design company dwp.

Scott attributes his interest in the Bangkok shophouse to his suburban upbringing in Australia, which engendered a hankering for the richness of urban living. He points out that today in Thailand shophouses are commonly seen as 'old-fashioned,

dark and second-class', fit only to be torn down and their land consolidated for high-rise office buildings or condominiums. But he saw the potential to recycle and redevelop them into contemporary urban homes. This would not only preserve buildings of character but also avoid the destruction of traditional street life and local communities.

Scott's house is located in a cul-de-sac right in the heart of Bangkok's business district. Part of a row of neglected 1980s faux Roman-style shop-

houses, it was typical of its kind—a simple concrete column and frame structure with brick infill walls with floors and windows that could be easily modified. While lending itself to adaptive reuse, the building typically brought with it certain challenges. Unlike the Chinese shophouse in Singapore or Malaysia, the Thai shophouse generally covers the entire site without a garden or an interior lightwell. It is dark with small rooms and windows and single brick party walls.

Left Scott Whittaker's converted shophouse is thoroughly transparent, maximizing natural light, but cleverly protecting it from direct sunlight.

Above left Long section.

Above right Front section.

Right The sleek and minimal lines of the kitchen support the transparency by drawing the eye through the house.

Keeping the existing structure of columns and beams, stair placement and existing slabs, Scott aimed to create a contemporary home that embodied the spirit of the original shophouse without attempting to replicate it—in other words, a contemporary urban house which in scale and character fitted in with its neighbours. This involved optimizing the amount of natural light and ventilation but minimizing direct sunlight. In addition, the design aimed to introduce greenery and outdoor spaces and to connect with the streetscape while still ensuring privacy. The best time to view this house is at night when it glows like a lantern and you can see the way it integrates both vertically and horizontally.

Comprising 400 square metres spread over four levels, the Bangkok House gives the impression of being one continuous space, with each level floating in a loose and easy relationship with the others. The front façade is a framed box with extruded blade walls and canopy, extending on one side as a green wall to provide privacy from the neighbour. This box frames the whole house, but acts primarily as a sunscreen. At the rear, the house 'borrows' a massive rain tree for sun protection. Because of the free-flowing spaces, sliding glass doors at the front and back ensure cross-ventilation. Vertically, air is drawn up through the house in a chimney effect by an industrial-style ventilator at the top of the stairs.

Scott Whittaker's home is really a very simple place with individual spaces merely indicated by furnishings or by minimal partitions. The master bathroom, for example, is hardly a bathroom at all with its free-standing bath sitting outside the shower recess more or less in the middle of the floor. Finishes have been kept to a minimum, and apart from some sanitary fixtures and travertine stone, all the materials have been locally sourced, including some recycled teakwood from an old Thai rice barn. The original slabs have been retained, except where sections have been cut out.

Spaces seem to float in a house which almost dematerializes, so it is surprising just how much intimacy and privacy is achieved, which includes

Left The sitting area embraces the neighbouring streetscape.

Right Even vertically, the house seems to dematerialize into a single flowing space.

Below Double-height sliding glass doors and the set back upper level ensure ample light.

clearly separate domains for the occupants and guests. Outdoor balconies and terraces are provided at both back and front, as well as a rooftop spa and a garden.

This is a project which is sustainable in the sense that it has been able to give new life to an old building, avoiding the cost and embodied energy of demolition and reconstruction. But it is also sustainable in the sense that it simultaneously rejuvenates and maintains the streetscape and the local community, demonstrating an alternative to developments which turn their back on the street and an authentic community. This is in addition to its use of natural light and ventilation, and its preference for locally sourced materials.

Above The free-standing bath signals how a sitting area and the bath area merge into one space.

Below Looking back through the dining room, the rain tree can be seen filtering morning sun.

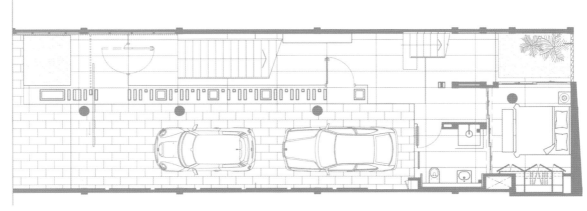

Above left The rooftop spa is a magically private and indulgent space.

Above right Light is drawn into the master bedroom through a small court.

Centre Ground floor plan.

Right A vertiginous view down to the street highlights the green blade wall at street level.

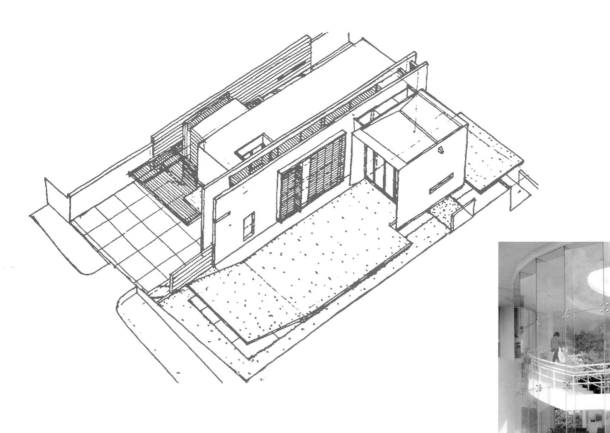

MALAYSIA

CARPHENIE HOUSE
KUALA LUMPUR, MALAYSIA
DESIGN COLLECTIVE ARCHITECTS

Above The Carphenie House dominates the landscape with its assertive sculptural quality.

Opposite above Ground floor plan.

Opposite below Entry from the street involves an arrival sequence that delays revealing the awe-inspiring entry void.

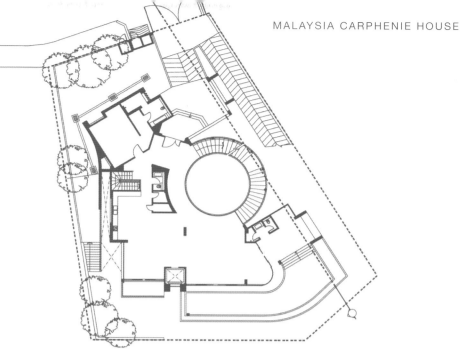

'When a client hires us, we shouldn't design *our* house, we should design *their* house. The house is an instrument for how they live.'—David Chan

Design Collective Architects (DCA) takes its 'client first' philosophy very seriously. Director David Chan explains that a new client is given 80 questions to answer, among them 'What are the five most important things in your life?' The aim is to uncover the client's values, which in turn helps the architects set up a productive triangular relationship between the client (user), the architect and the site (land).

In this case, the clients were a mother and her daughter who are both medical practitioners in Hong Kong. Having friends in Kuala Lumpur, they fell in love with the city, its lifestyle and its food. Although they continue to live and work in Hong Kong, this house is their refuge for several months of the year. 'The objective', says David Chan, 'was to be able to live opposite to the way they live in Hong Kong—to get out of the pressure cooker.' In other words, the house sustains them in the way in which it compensates for an intense professional life in an intense city. It gives the occupants all the things they don't have in Hong Kong—space, light, greenery, privacy and fresh air.

At the same time, there is a reassuring sense of connection with the clients' life in Hong Kong because the clean lines and the dominating white palette, along with the clear and simple circulation, have the clinical purity of a hospital. Even the vinyl flooring in the entry court curves up the wall at the edges to make for easy cleaning—just as in a hospital. But this soft and seamless flooring highlights a key issue for the clients. It is durable

and easy to clean. This is a house which is not occupied for lengthy periods, so it needs to be easily maintained.

The house is located in a gated community on the outskirts of Kuala Lumpur. It sits on an elevated site with sweeping views across a small man-made lake and a golf course. One of the drivers of the design was to take full advantage of this panoramic outlook, enjoy the spatial freedom and build in lots of transparency.

Director Chan Mun Inn points out that when you enter the door in a traditional Asian house, you are in the house. The architects did not want that here, so they have created an awesome transitional space—a circular internal courtyard open to the sky, with a grassy mound and garden and a tree reaching for the sky. A terrazzo surround protects the rest of the entry floor from the rain.

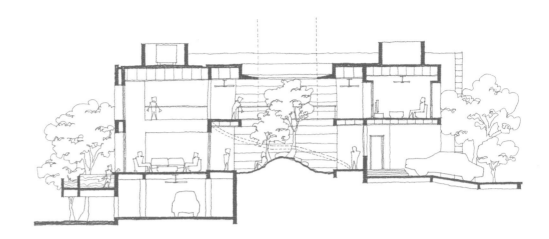

Above The vortical experience of the house is echoed by the sweeping grand staircase.

Right A view from the mezzanine.

Above left Section drawing.

Left The entry void spills into grand perimeter spaces.

The ground floor is the public area. Once inside the internal courtyard, one can turn back and around to the right to access the guest bedroom or proceed straight ahead to the open-plan kitchen, dining and living area. The dry kitchen is the only one, the clients preferring not to have a wet kitchen, partly because they felt it would lead to a waste of food given their love of eating out. The living room is a double-height space which can be viewed from the gallery on the upper level and is connected to the court by sliding glass doors. It has a grand view across the golf course through a fully glazed wall and a small balcony. The living room includes a curved, glazed corner lounge to sit in and enjoy the view. It also accesses a deck to the J-shaped infinity-edge swimming pool.

The form of the house is powerfully curvilinear. This form is generated by the circular internal courtyard, but it also takes advantage of the

trapezoid shape of the site which fans out at the back, maximizing the outlook. Being completely white—all the colour comes from the carpets and the furnishings—and so transparent, the house seems to dematerialize, becoming one with the view. In this way, it fulfils one of the clients' key requirements, namely, not to have to turn on a light or the air-conditioning during the day. The house is thus bathed in natural light, and with its elevated position and openness is able to capture any breeze and generate cross-ventilation.

The upstairs private spaces are accessed by an imposing spiral stairway. Its handrail, which is lit from beneath by LED lighting, becomes a decorative feature at night.

A circular gallery at the top of the stairway generates the circulation of the upper level, which includes three bedrooms and a family lounge. The master bedroom enjoys the main view over the

Above The clinical white of the house is offset by the bold colours of the furnishings and accessories.

Left The modernist kitchen, which also serves as a breakfast bar.

Opposite above left The ground floor sitting room provides a good view of the pool.

Opposite above right The main living area seen from the mezzanine.

Right The main living area on the streetside of the house.

golf course with operable blinds for privacy. Like the rest of the house, the master bathroom is highly transparent with a Roman bath in the middle and a wall of sliding mirrored doors. A feature of both the main bedrooms is the provision of male and female toilets.

Unusually for Malaysia, DCA routinely uses cavity walls for all exterior walls, which has the benefit of reducing heat penetration. There is also a curved free-standing wall on the western side that screens the house from the western sun and provides privacy from the neighbouring house by masking the master bathroom and the daughter's bedroom, allowing the windows to be left permanently open.

This wall also creates a wind tunnel to generate cross-ventilation for the side of the house which is otherwise less exposed to breezes.

This house, then, is highly sustainable in terms of its low maintenance and high levels of natural light, cross-ventilation and heat exclusion. But it has also been designed to provide emotional sustenance because it acts as a refuge for its occupants, giving them the amenities they lack when working in high-density Hong Kong.

Above left The j-shaped pool continues the curvilinear theme of the house.

Above right The entry void, with its elegant curved wall and circular stone fringe to the central garden, has a temple-like feel.

Opposite above left and below The curved free-standing wall generates natural ventilation and provides screening from the sun and from neighbours.

Far right The circular entry void culminates in a grand oculus open to the sky.

KUBIK HOUSE
IPOH, MALAYSIA
MARRA + YEH

Right Entry to the house seen from the street.

Below Entry level and lower level plans.

Opposite The long cooking/eating bench is designed for entertaining large numbers of people.

'Why do people want to live in houses and then live as though they were living in apartments? It defeats the purpose. They want a garden and they want a house, but then they close it all up.'—Carol Marra

Marra + Yeh have always been fascinated by the tension between what architects are trying to achieve and what craftsmen can actually make. Working a great deal in Malaysia, they are acutely aware of what is available and what is possible. 'What we try to do in our designs', says Marra, 'is to take your normal construction methods and normal materials and think of some way to modify them so that they increase the environmental perform-ance of the building.'

She points out that these solutions can be sophisticated without being outrageously expensive or involve high-tech machinery, or control systems 'which people either can't afford or can't understand or are not even available in that country'.

In developing their approach to sustainable tropical living, Marra + Yeh have been strongly influenced by expatriate Danish architect Berthel Michael Iversen who established an office in Ipoh in 1934. As well as incorporating vernacular references in his otherwise modernist buildings, Iversen developed a range of strategies for natural ventilation and sun control, and also made use of local materials in innovative ways.

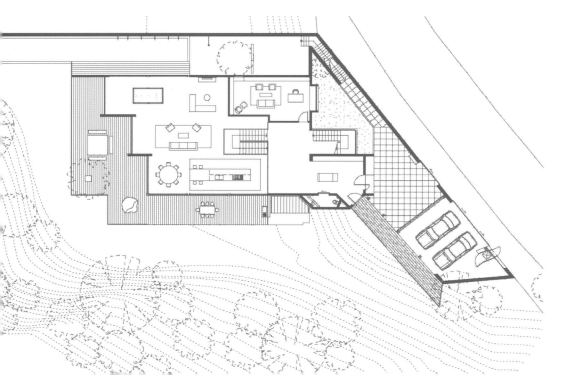

There is not a lot that is typical about the Kubik House. The client is a German precision engineer married to a Malaysian Chinese, who wanted to escape from the formality of Europe and live a relaxed lifestyle with a strong connection to nature. He also did not want a 'typical Malaysian house'.

Where everybody else was looking for a flat, rectangular site, he chose one that was trapezoidal in shape with a steep slope falling three metres—making half the site unsuitable for building—and a stream running down the side. The architects saw opportunities in the site.

The initial brief was for an informal house where all the doors could be left open, with space to entertain and room for their extended Malaysian family and long-term guests from Europe. Later, the client asked for an office where he could receive business associates without them having to go through the house.

The result is a response to at least three things. First, it was a response to the topography. Secondly, it was a response to the macro and micro climate and issues such as wind and sun. Thirdly, it was a response to the challenge of how to simultaneously

provide privacy and community within the same house. In other words, they set out to design a home that was physically and culturally of its place.

In the end, it was the topography of the site that facilitated the programme for the house. The house is built over three levels and follows the fall of the slope. Arrival is at the middle level where there is an entry platform with the client's office off to the side. This is the *public space*. From there one either goes upstairs to the bedrooms and the *private space* or downstairs to the glazed, double-height *communal space*.

Opposite The living/dining/cooking area looking back to the stairs leading from the entry.

Left and below The living/dining area enjoys full transparency to the garden and forest outside. Its customized folding timber and glass doors create one continuous space from inside to the outside terrace, which wraps around two sides of the house.

There is thus a sense of journeying through the house—a journey which actually begins from the roadside where there is little sense of what the building is really like. In the transition from the public to the private realm, the house only reveals itself gradually. Indeed, it never reveals all of itself at any one time. 'It is', says Carol Marra, 'about what you present to the public face and what you keep to yourself.'

Apart from its connection with nature and the provision of a generous entertainment area, the expansive living/dining/entertainment space on the lower level also plays an important role in climate control.

All the doors and windows can open, but during the hottest part of the day the double-height volume allows hot air to rise and be drawn up through the stairwell, thus creating constant air movement. Unlike most buildings in the tropics, this house (because of the site) is oriented south–north, which enabled the architects to harness the prevailing winds and funnel air through the house.

Right The living/dining space looks directly out to a heavily forested steep slope with a cascading stream.

The topography also assisted climate control in another intriguing way. Above the house is a 500-metre hill, while 300 metres below is a pond. During the evenings, a cloud of moist air settles over the site, moving down towards the pond. In the morning, this cloud begins to move up again, creating the equivalent of a sea breeze.

Other climate control devices in the Kubik House include refurbished 1940s General Electric fans and an evaporative cooler developed in the United States. Unlike air-conditioners, the evaporative process takes place inside the machine, hence it is not adding moisture to already saturated tropical air. It does use a lot of water though, about 8 litres an hour, but this is supplied from an underground water storage tank fed from the roof. The air comes out of the cooler at about 26 degrees Centigrade, depending on how dry it is outside. The exhaust is pushed out to two air-compressors, which sustain the only air-conditioning in the house, located in the bedrooms. By pushing the cool saturated air into the compressors, the compressors work less because the ambient temperature is reduced. Hence, the air-conditioning itself is made more energy-efficient.

The air control system in the house works in tandem with the wall construction. Unlike the normal double-brick wall construction, this house has an outer skin of brick and an inner skin of aerated, lightweight concrete blocks with a layer of aluminium foil placed in between. The effect is to push heat out but also to absorb cool air on the inside. So, instead of cooling air, it is a thermal mass (the concrete block wall) which is being cooled. This acts like a battery, retaining the cool air. Tests showed that the room stayed at about 24 degrees until 3.00 pm in the afternoon—a huge energy saving compared to normal air-conditioning.

The project was also an exercise in sustaining local crafts and materials. A local craftsman who makes dragon heads out of rattan for Chinese New Year was commissioned to make the frames for custom-designed pendant lamps which were then pasted up with Chinese linen and Japanese paper. The stone flooring in the living area and bathrooms is local Ipoh marble, while all the timber is air-dried waste timber from a local flooded dam site. All the doors and windows are timber within steel frames. Local joiners were used to make the frames which fit perfectly despite the zero tolerance of the steel frames.

German and Malaysian Chinese clients bring together two quite different concepts of privacy and community. Where private space may be a high priority for a Westerner, Asian cultures are more communal and will tend to have more fluid spaces. The Kubik House aims to reconcile these two tendencies by providing both private and communal spaces, but linking them in a fluid way.

Right One of two geese that wander freely around the site.
Below Long elevation.
Bottom left The outside terrace which 'floats' above the tumbling landscape.
Bottom right The steepness of the site can be seen from the car port at street level.

Above The entry vestibule with the home office/client reception on the right.

Right The angled, soaring street elevation provides no hint of the dramatic interior spatial organization.

Far left The pool, which runs the length of the living/dining space.

Above, centre and bottom left The street elevation has a De Stijl quality with its modernistic arrangement of geometrical forms and high contrast colours.

HOUSE AT DAMANSARA
KUALA LUMPUR
RT+Q ARCHITECTS

"This house was a labour of love. It started as a passion and ended as a passion."—Rene Tan

It is really the story of two houses. The client already owned a house on the adjacent block, an exquisite modern reinterpretation of the tropical house by Soo K. Chan from SCDA. After acquiring the neighbouring property and demolishing the existing house, he asked Rene Tan to design a 'biggish-looking small house' in its place that would complement the Soo Chan house, duplicating the spaces in the original house but at a scale which would accommodate expanded entertainment. Having lived in a rather tropical house, the client now wanted to live in 'something more modern' but with as much garden area as possible.

Rene Tan's solution is what he calls 'a modern rendition of a tropical, naturally ventilated house'. The challenge was to make the new house different but still relate it to the existing house, especially as there is a one level difference between the two sites. The old house is now aligned with the basement of the new house, with the two houses back to back.

Interestingly, the difference in level seems to connect the two houses rather than separate them. Although the new house was seen initially as an 'annex' to the old one, it is now the old house which seems like the annex—a kind of gracious, quiet refuge whose low light levels are a meditative contrast to the light-drenched new house. With Rene Tan—a trained musician—it is always apposite to use musical metaphors. One could say that the old house is like a gentle, introspective slow movement which follows a grand and extroverted opening movement.

But in subtle ways the two houses have a close affinity. The elegant, free-flowing plan of the original house with its 'verandah rooms' is paralleled in the new house, but with an infusion of natural light and the presence of the awe-inspiring double-height living space with an entire wall of Carrara marble. 'This', says Tan, 'is the big event of the house'—the *finale* of the symphony—which opens up both to the south and to the north where it overlooks the original house. Double-height sliding glass doors on either side maximize cross-ventilation, while deep overhangs optimize sun protection.

Apart from the 'big event', the new house has its own special intimacy to reflect that of the original house. The house is L-shaped with the core forming the long leg and the living space the short leg. The core consists of a long circulation spine expressed through two commanding parallel, double-height walls. Public spaces, which include a powder room-cum-swimming pool changing room and a dry kitchen and dining space opening on to the 20-metre swimming pool, are on the ground floor level, along with the bedrooms of the client's two sons. The master bedroom is on the upper level.

With the new house, the architects—the design team included T. K. Quek and Tan Shen Ru in addition to Rene Tan—set out to create a more abstract form of 'tropical modern'. The aim was to incorporate the sun protection and natural ventilation strategies of the traditional tropical house, but to otherwise embody the spirit of the tropical house rather than imitate its outward form.

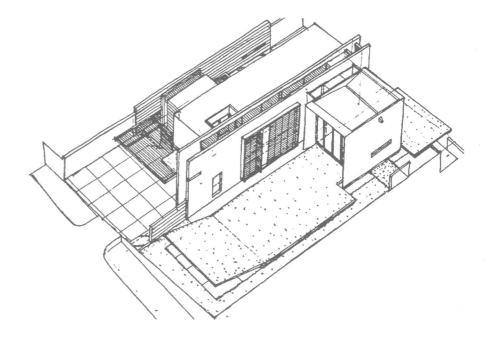

Left This view down into the music/sitting room is from a small 'Juliet' balcony.

Below left A box frame extrudes from the music/sitting room to provide protection from the sun.

Right The galleria leads from the entry and acts a spine for a series of entertainment rooms and bedrooms, all facing on to the pool.

Opposite below left Ground floor plan.

Opposite below right The view from the galleria into an entertainment room with its own dry kitchen and bar.

The house is mainly made of fair-faced concrete, white plaster and paint. But the use of dark-toned framing, dark timber-battened screens and black granite and walnut timber floors creates an affinity of palette with the old house.

The circulation spine is a kind of gallery enclosed on both levels on the garden side by a wall of dark-timbered pivoting louvred panels. Yes, it does let the rain in, but as Tan says, 'In the tropics, you have to put up with certain inconveniences. This is not', he goes on, 'an air-conditioned house.'

The house balances entertainment areas with relatively modest domestic amenities—just three bedrooms. The master bedroom suite is, however, quite grand in conception, with oak veneer wall linings and a huge glass-walled walk-in wardrobe. The big feature of the bathroom is the free-standing bath in the middle of the room set within its own open pavilion, which Tan describes as 'a building within a building'.

The total land area is 10,000 square feet with a built-up area of 7,000 square feet. That means quite a lot of space has been retained as garden. Given that the brief was for a 'biggish-looking small house', the house needed to have 'an attitude', says Tan. But the brief also called for a large garden area. To maximize the garden, the architects kept it flat but lifted it a little to 'give it presence'. Instead of five little gardens, says Tan, they designed one big one. On the eastern side, this is basically an expanse of

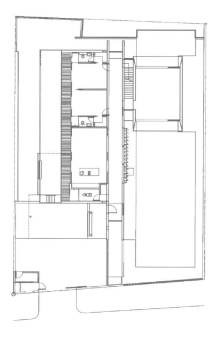

lawn leading down to the living pavilion. On the western side, the garden is more intimate, accommodating a 20-metre swimming pool continually refreshed by fountains and a waterfall and framed on the other side of the lawn by a 20-metre-long black granite wall with water coursing down its textured surface.

Reconciling privacy with connection to the outside, marrying one way of life (in the original house) with another (in the new house), and maximizing access to natural light and natural ventilation make this house sustainable in more than one sense of the word.

Above A wilderness of mirrors reveals the opulent 'bath house' and bathroom off the master bedroom.

Below The master bedroom's interior timber finishes complement the dark-stained louvre doors that form a 'verandah room' and allow natural ventilation without compromising privacy.

Below The bathrooms and powder rooms express a luxury which is only hinted at in the more restrained public areas of the house.

Opposite above Looking from the entertainment room to the pool.

Left The side garden is a series of planes—deck, pool, lawn and black granite water wall.

TING HOUSE
KUALA LUMPUR, MALAYSIA
WOOI ARCHITECT

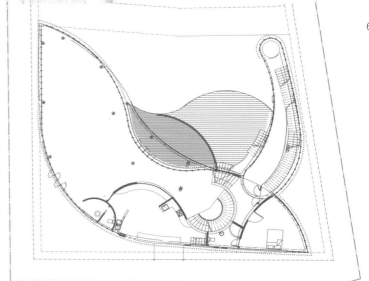

Left The house responds to the dramatic topography of a site which the architect saw as more of an opportunity than a challenge.

Above right Plan of the ground floor, including the main living area.

Below The curved form of the house wraps a protective arm around part of the outdoor entertainment deck.

'The idea behind the Ting House is to renew a sense of wonder in the familiarity of living in an equatorial zone by judicious framing and limiting the view, light, shadow, breeze, sky and surroundings. Working with the curvaceous contour and the steep sloping site accentuates the spatial experience as one moves about the space vertically and horizontally.'—Lok Kuang Wooi

This house is part of a gated community located in a former rubber plantation. The hilly topography gives the house a sense of privacy and exclusivity, while also offering some splendid panoramas.

The clients are a couple with two grown-up children who had previously lived in semi-detached and terrace houses and now wanted something more individual and independent. When they invited architect Lok Kuang Wooi to look at the development site, very few of the lots had been sold. They were therefore surprised when he chose a site set on a steep slope where the access road is 15 metres below the back boundary and 11 metres below the first buildable level.

But the architect saw an opportunity to build a distinctive building that grew out of the landscape and took advantage of the views. He also saw the opportunity to create a contemporary tropical house which in form, palette and materials was a part of its natural context and which worked with the climate, not against it. Hence, the elevated siting of the building enables such a high degree of natural ventilation that the owners rarely have to use air-conditioning.

In addition, the extended curving elevation of the house as it follows the contour of the hill allowed for a shallow floorplate, ensuring that natural light penetrates every part of the house. The marked elevation of the house above the road also guarantees privacy, allowing the house to be fully transparent, even the bedrooms and bathrooms. The owners thus feel permanently connected to the outside landscape.

Finally, the house offers significant spatial experiences, both vertically and horizontally, once

66

again reflecting the experience of living in a rugged tropical terrain.

The basic curve of the house follows the contour of the hill and defines, on the first level or ground floor, the main body of the house—the living, dining and kitchen areas. Outside, there is a spa terrace and a *koi* pond. The wall and floor of the spa utilize rock taken from the site.

The front wall of the living and dining areas consists of full-height glass with sliding doors. Here, instead of the usual concrete columns, the architect has used clusters of slender load-bearing steel pipes which contribute to the overall 'industrial' feel of the house. But this industrial feel is tempered by the use of timber, especially the vertical 1 x 2" *chengal* hardwood screen which rises from the

Above The vertiginous stairwell of concrete is both alarming and exciting.

Left The curved wall that partly masks the main living area from the top of the stairs.

Below Entry to the living/dining area is a counterpoint of concrete, local brick, steel and glass.

Above The hardwood screen provides privacy without excluding light or access to views.

Left The clusters of steel supporting tubes hint at the tall trees outside.

Below The spacious master bedroom.

lower ground level to the roof eave. The delicate filigree nature of the screen complements the robust concrete structure of the building, while the material and the palette help it blend into the landscape. It also acts as a sun filter, reducing heat and softening the light. In parts, it also acts as a railing and as a security grill.

A secondary curved volume begins at street level next to the garage. This houses the entry stairway, gallery and gymnasium and also provides privacy for the decks in the event of the adjacent plot being developed.

There are few arrival sequences to rival the one at the Ting House. From the garage at street level, the visitor passes through a solid timber door—originally intended to be a table top—into a stairwell to proceed up a heady spiral staircase comprising 56 steps. (There is also a lift for the less able-bodied.) At the upper ground floor, there is a naturally lit landing followed by another nine steps before the visitor emerges into the grand space of the living area, although this view is initially modulated by the curved wall of the kitchen, thus giving the space a dynamic, flowing character.

Above This view of the deck gives an indication of the panoramas afforded by the elevated siting of the house.

Above right Organic curved shapes constantly meet and separate.

The curving motif of the external form of the building is thus mirrored inside the house, both on the living/dining level and on the top floor. Here there are three family bedrooms and a guest room, together with a gymnasium.

In many ways, this is a house of journeys, both vertical and horizontal. Going up the stairs engenders a slight frisson of anxiety because, although the stairs are made from concrete, they are also remarkably delicate. But one is led ever upward, lured by the vision of a rich and beautifully detailed timber ceiling. Once inside the house proper, the spaces flow into one another without fully revealing themselves until the last minute.

Left Concealed lighting in the stairway creates the impression of a ritual journey.

Below left At the top of the entry stairs, a galleria leads to the gymnasium.

Below A timber screen turns the spa into an intimate bathing pavilion.

Bottom The section reveals how the house 'occupies' the hill.

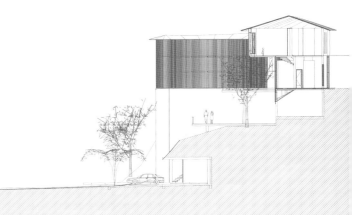

Left The free-standing bath in the master bathroom reflects the 'industrial' feel of the house.

Right The stairway, with its soaring, organic space, can seem almost Gothic.

Below The curved stairway from the public spaces to the private areas.

Opposite The gallery arm of the house curves around to provide privacy from any future development next door.

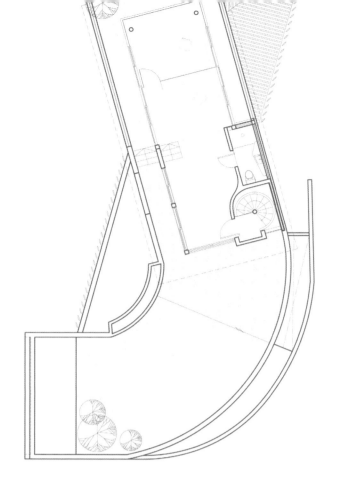

SINGAPORE

BROOKVALE APARTMENT
SINGAPORE
TRISTAN AND JULIANA STUDIO

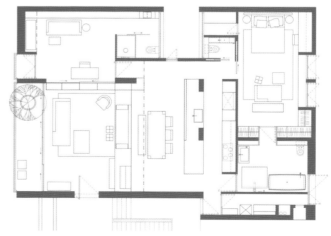

Left The balcony has been opened up to become an extension of the living room.

Below left The floor plan reveals how the apartment has become an assemblage of free-flowing spaces.

Right Removal of the ceiling has exposed the trusses, which have become a decorative feature in what is now a very generous space.

'One would be hard pressed to find equivalent sophistication in the modern designs of today. Walk-up apartment blocks as old as Brookvale are an endangered species in our city-country of Singapore.'—Juliana Chan

This top floor corner apartment is part of a 1980s apartment block on the western side of Singapore. The area is lush and attractively landscaped, creating the impression of a self-contained community precinct. The apartment block itself sits on a hill and backs on to the dense jungle of the Maju military base reserve.

They might not have the heritage caché of the shophouse, but walk-up apartment blocks from the Brookvale Park era can mount an equally strong case for preservation and renewal. First, in their design and use of materials, they have architectural character. Secondly, in terms of their internal planning, says architect Juliana Chan, 'they combine both a stroke of practicality in their economy of scale, whilst maintaining sensitivity to the spatial proportions and distances required for its inhabitants to live life without the intrusive pressure of urbanity.'

The generous balcony and ingenious spatial organization were two things that persuaded Juliana Chan and her interior designer husband Tristan Tan, who previously ran Singapore's popular furniture showroom Cream, that the apartment had the potential for reinvention. The result is a strong argument for 'recycling' existing apartment buildings rather than the more common practice of demolition and rebuilding, which often ends up with apartment buildings that are claustrophobic, formulaic and much less sensitive to their physical and historical context.

Like the many shophouse make-overs, this Brookvale Park apartment is an instructive exercise

in how an existing dwelling can be adapted to a sophisticated contemporary lifestyle without losing the character and sense of community which come with its history.

Other sustainable aspects of this renovation include opening up the interior and rethinking the fenestration to promote cross-ventilation, and generating a greater sense of connection with the outside, especially at the rear of the apartment where the new master bedroom and bathroom both 'borrow' the landscape of the reserve without any loss of privacy.

Being on the top floor of the building offered a crucial advantage. By removing the artificial ceiling, the designers were able to exploit the sharply pitched roof of the building to significantly increase the volumes in the apartment, especially in the living/dining/kitchen area in the front part. This exercise revealed the timber rafters, which were sanded back and restored. In this way, not only is the sense of space in the apartment greatly enhanced but the intrinsic character of the building is revealed.

The internal spaces have also been thoroughly rethought so that the apartment now has a public area (living/dining/kitchen), a private area (bedroom and bathroom) and an in-between space (home office). The latter is on the same level as the kitchen and bedroom, about a metre above the entry level and living space, and was formerly the master bedroom. It is an in-between space because the dividing wall has been removed and replaced by see-through shelving to partially connect it to the living space.

The public area begins at the entry with the living area that leads out to the balcony. A settee, which faces the balcony, is integrated into a series of floating steps that lead from the stone floor of the living area to the timber floor of the kitchen/dining area. The elevation of the kitchen/dining area makes the living space seem like a sunken den, a cosy self-contained space which avoids any sense of claustrophobia because of the wide balcony doors, and by being visually connected to the rear of the apartment by doorways on either side of the kitchen unit and to the studio.

The long quartz benchtop and elegantly integrated, linear kitchen joinery serve to separate the public and private areas. Originally, the rear of the apartment contained two guest bedrooms, a kitchen and a service bath. This has been rationalized into a single bedroom with an en suite. (There is also a powder room and small storeroom adjacent to the kitchen.) The bedroom ceiling was also removed to expose the timber trusses and sloping roof, and the bedroom was connected to the bathroom by a concealed door in the dark timber built-in wardrobe.

Just as the bedroom borrows the outside landscape, the bathroom has the character of an outdoor room with a free-standing bath and a Boffi tubular shower, which stands in the middle of the floor without a screen—all looking out to the reserve through a generously sized window.

The finishes and furnishings in the apartment have all been carefully selected and crafted to combine contemporary taste with the slightly rustic character of the original building. Hence, the tables

and stools are from e15, the dining chairs are Hans Wegner 'Wishbone', the sofa bed is Gervasoni and the kitchen appliances are all Miele. Other furnishings, however, are either restored antique pieces or have been custom-designed to lend a homely, spontaneous feel.

Similarly, other elements help maintain a historical connection through their materials and palette. The frame around the kitchen unit, for example, is CorTen steel, and there is a range of timber palette from light to dark. The external window frames are pre-rusted steel to hint at the original framing, while the internal glazing is very contemporary.

This apartment is an outstanding example of adaptive reuse. Demolition and rebuilding have been avoided and the inherent character of the apartment has been explored to create a stylish contemporary dwelling. In the process, the apartment has been rethought to meet the needs of a young couple without children whose professional background reflects the changing face of Singapore.

Opposite The transparency of the bookcase, with a view through to the elevated home office, helps dispel any sense of confinement.

Left The 'stage' of the dining area also gives the opportunity for a banquette and some elegant floating steps to the upper level.

Above The private area is behind the kitchen pod and includes a powder room and laundry.

Below The view of the living area from the elevated kitchen/dining space shows the entry door and reveals how the small apartment now has a feeling of spaciousness.

THE COPPER HOUSE
SENTOSA, SINGAPORE
CSYA

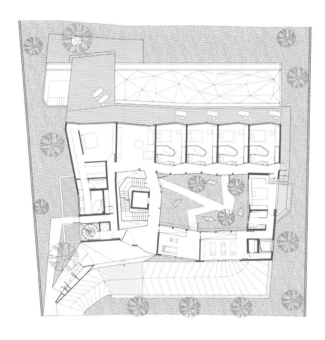

'It has been quite a painful process. Not because of the client, but because of the design. There is not a single surface that is straight.'—Sonny Chan

This is a house which never stands still. Look at it from the front (the street), look at it from the back (the ocean promenade) or, indeed, from up on its surging green roof, and the house is in constant motion. There is no fixed point of view to tell us where this house begins and where it ends.

Inside, it is the same story, as the house constantly unfolds into something else in a kind of magical mystery tour, an Alice in Wonderland-type experience where nothing is what it seems.

Architect Sonny Chan says they set out to design a monolith and this is what it is. While there are multiple perspectives, they all combine to form a seamless unity.

The house is made from concrete, but dressed in a copper skin—which may be hot to the touch in the tropical heat, but it also has thermal properties which moderate heat penetration. It therefore collaborates with the high levels of cross-ventilation to minimize the need for air-conditioning.

The cross-ventilation is generated by the fact that the house is effectively just one room deep, since it wraps around an interior garden courtyard with only an operable glass louvred corridor separating the bedrooms on the ground floor from the internal court and, on the ocean side, with sliding glass doors connecting the bedrooms directly to the pool, the Jacuzzi and the garden.

Above The ground floor plan shows the dynamic irregularity of the planning.

Right On the waterside elevation of the house, a grassy berm provides privacy from the public walkway.

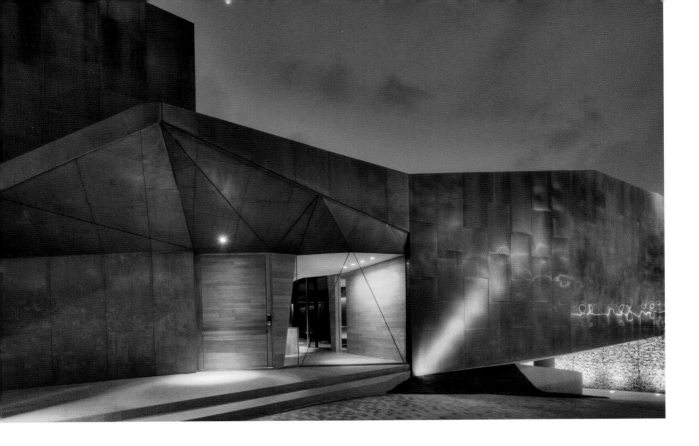

The strategy was to optimize exposure to the sea breezes. Since the sea is ten metres away and then three metres beneath the promenade, it was decided to place all the bedrooms on the ground floor and the dining and entertainment spaces on the next level to enjoy not just the sea breezes but also the sweeping ocean views.

The things which promote natural ventilation also maximize natural light and lower dependency on artificial lighting. This is done in conjunction with the quirky sculptural character of the house. The eccentric faceted glass prisms which seem to have dropped randomly from the sky into the garden courtyard actually draw light down into the basement car park.

As the architects point out, the house 'evolves' from the ground floor up in a vortical fashion. This ultimately leads to the green rooftop which, from its access point, continues to climb by way of a spiral timber walkway to the summit, culminating in a timber terrace, ideal for cocktails at sunset. This roof, inspired by that of the Yokohama

international passenger terminal, really does seem like the end of a journey which involves the house transforming from an opaque monolith (albeit with delicate perforations to the copper screen) through increasing transparency until at the summit it becomes one with the sea and the sky. It celebrates this connection with a rolling green lawn that might be artificial grass but which nonetheless provides an additional insulating skin to assist with internal climate control.

In fact, the house *is* a journey—a vortical or spiralling progression which makes it simultaneously a horizontal and a vertical journey. This begins at the ground floor entry where one is immediately confronted by what Chan calls the *pièce de résistance*, the lift, which is housed in a science fiction-like sculptural pod of faceted bronze-coloured stainless steel. This is the first example of many where the vorticist character of the journey through the house is also expressed in three dimensions—as with the irregularly shaped internal courtyard, the garden skylights, even the

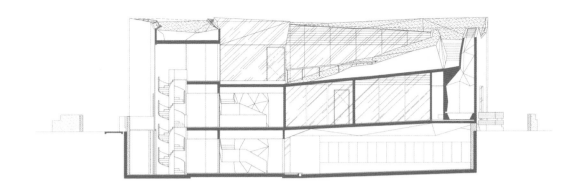

Left The street entry to the house immediately signals the intriguing nature of the house.

Below left The internal garden courtyard is completely irregular, including the sculptural glass prisms that draw light into the basement car park.

Right The section reveals how the house is every bit as dynamic vertically as it is horizontally.

Below The bedrooms along the waterside elevation each have direct access to the swimming pool and open up to sea breezes.

gabion retaining wall in the basement car park, which also reduces the need for cement.

The lift is a sculptural object that blocks any immediate view into the house or beyond to the ocean view. The garden courtyard is glimpsed to the right, while beyond the lift core is the master bedroom and bathroom and a sitting room.

Although this is basically a weekender, not a permanent home, the children are given their own wing with its own entry and the bedrooms opening individually on to the glass louvred corridor. However, even the children enjoy amenities which Chan quips are 'pretty luxe'. Their bedrooms open directly on to the pool, with bathrooms screened by translucent glass and benches of onyx marble, along with the aged-textured, wire-brushed oak wall finishes.

Above The master bedroom.

Left The eccentric sculptural bronze lift core inside the entry.

Above right A wine storage unit forms an elegant room divider between the main living room and the dining area on the second floor.

Right The entertainment room on the second level.

Far right The bathroom, spa and steam room have a ritualistic quality.

Right The glazed corridor linking the children's bedrooms looks into the central court.

Centre right The sculptural drama is exemplified by the staircase.

Far right After the initial surprise of the lift core, there is another one as it descends, following the staircase, to the basement.

Below right A small sitting room on the ground floor adjacent to the garden court.

Left The dining area on the second level has a breakfast bar and food preparation facilities.

Below Finishes throughout are exquisite and varied.

Beyond the children's bedrooms is a darkly handsome bathroom, spa and steam room adjacent to a massage room where the perforated copper skin casts a calming dappled light.

Upstairs is the dining room with an underlit onyx floor and the entertainment room, separated from the dining space by a powder room. This whole level opens up to the view and the sea breezes.

'We try to tell our clients', says Chan, 'that you can live without air-conditioning.' Like the other Sentosa houses which front the sea, this is certainly achievable in this house where there is a constant sea breeze to be captured. The shallow depth of the house, along with the permeability of generous opening glass windows and doors, ensures that the house is constantly ventilated.

The house is also a reminder, albeit on an opulent scale, that holiday houses play an important role in bringing families together. During the working week, everyone has something else to do. With a house designed to sustain family life, at the weekend or on holiday they can again become a family unit.

Left The waterside elevation seen from the public walkway.

Below The textured copper skin wraps around the form of the house, with the reflecting glass feature window next to the entry providing the first of many surprises.

Above The pathway to the 'summit' of the roof garden offers a visual reprise of the house looking back down to the garden court.

Left The timber path to the summit and the green roof replicate the eccentric forms below.

Below The viewing deck and barbeque at the summit.

FOURTH AVENUE HOUSE
SINGAPORE
RICHARD HO ARCHITECTS

Right Seen from the street, the house sits like a temple on a hill.

Bottom The section reveals how the house steps up in levels.

Opposite The idea of climbing steps to a temple is echoed in the concrete faceting of the pool terrace.

'Sustainable and green design has to begin with the design, not by buying technology. This house is unique in that all the spaces, except for the bedrooms, are designed for natural ventilation, with no air-conditioning, and almost all the materials used are recycled or recyclable. It is an evolution of the black-and-white house with no apologies for its cultural origin.'—Richard Ho

The Fourth Avenue House is designed for three generations. The owner is a return client who wanted a house which would be unique to him and which would carry over some of the character and memories of his old house. At the same time, it was to be a modern home, appropriate in every way to a highly successful businessman.

It was a perfect assignment for Richard Ho whose name is synonymous in Singapore for both quality heritage work and his ability to reconcile contemporary needs with cultural continuity. 'The architect',

says Ho, 'is a facilitator of the transition to the modern world, to the acquisition of taste.' Part of this role, he adds, is to help imbue his Asian clients with a sense of confidence of being in the modern world—'without the need for a Prada handbag'.

Although the house is a new build, it offered Ho the opportunity to explore ways of generating personal and cultural continuity, nowhere better illustrated than in the circular window with its inserted traditional Chinese carved square window in the main stairwell, and with the carved timber highlight windows connecting the living and entertainment rooms with the dining area.

But before this house became an example of person and cultural continuity, it was an exercise in environmental sustainability. It is situated in a cul-de-sac and on a steeply sloping site with a drop of three metres. From the street, the site steps up the hillside, giving the house, with its wide eaves,

porticoed entry and verandah and granite pool steps, a temple-like aura and inviting the visitor to make his way up several flights of ceremonial stairs.

The site is also in a tree conservation area where all 40 of the existing trees have been retained to contribute to a lush garden setting. Its prominent high position not only gives the house sensational views over the city but also the opportunity to capture breezes. Ho has exploited this by creating expansive verandahs sheltered by wide eaves, and ensuring that the dining, living and entertainment spaces, all well set back, are effectively 'outdoor rooms' because they are all fully connected to the outside by large sliding doors which disappear into the walls. The cross-ventilation is so effective that air-conditioning is unnecessary in these downstairs spaces. 'You feel like you are living in a pavilion,' says Ho.

The wrap-around verandah, with its reconstituted granite columns and generous eaves giving protection from the sun and rain, is deliberately contrived to elicit memories of colonial black-and-white houses, while the courtyard screens and dining area hint at the Chinese courtyard house. This cultural reference is reinforced by the carved

Above The private areas on the top level of the main pavilion.

Below left The first storey plan again hints at a temple with a plan that suggests the Katsura Imperial Villa in Kyoto, Japan.

Below The void looking down into the dining area from the upper level private areas.

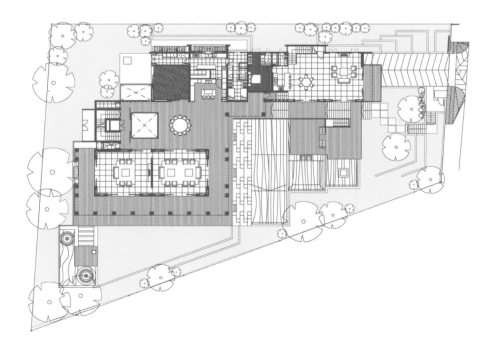

Above The traditional square within a circle window in the stairway reminds the occupants of their previous home.

Left The ornamental carved timber screen masks the lift and private areas from the public areas.

timber screen at the rear of the dining area, which rises up through an atrium space, masking the lift, separating the private and public domains and creating a vertical connection between the three levels of the house—besides conjuring up the memory of a Chinese shophouse.

Timber figures prominently throughout this 25,000-square foot house. Different woods are used for the courtyard screens, windows and atrium screen. Recycled timber is used to clad the house, for the dining area interior, and for the decking and flooring, using different treatments and assembled to create visual variety. The granite and timber theme is continued throughout. In the master bathroom, for example, a single slab of peach tree, a native of China that bears a variety of Chinese cultural associations, forms a bench, while the free-standing shower is granite-lined.

Right The huge custom-designed circular dining table sits not so much in a dining room as in a spacious deck linked to the living areas and a dry kitchen and breakfast bar.

Opposite below The main living area opens up completely to the terrace and garden on one side and the dining space on the other.

Left The children's wing steps down into a lush garden.

Below The living room draws on the colonial bungalow model with its deeply recessed verandahs and direct connection with the wrap-around terrace.

The public spaces are all located on the entry level whereas the private areas are on the top level, with the parents in the main pavilion and the children in the side wing. If, for the guest, the sense of arrival has a ceremonial quality to it, for the inhabitants it is a sense of homecoming, which begins with the four-car garage followed by entry into the atrium with its black granite pond. This bottom level also contains a home entertainment room.

The clear separation of public and private spaces in the Fourth Avenue House has allowed architect Richard Ho to create a wonderful feeling of refuge and prospect on the arrival level. Here, there is internal prospect as the kitchen, living, dining, entertainment and verandah spaces all flow easily from one to the other. At the same, all these spaces are directly connected with the outside landscape, drawing the eye first to the lawn and trees, then to the city beyond.

Left The home office.

Right The master bedroom.

Below The master bathroom is quietly opulent with its perfectly balanced selection of complementary materials.

Opposite The orderly, stepped arrival sequence of the external stairway mirrors the more complex stepping of the pools.

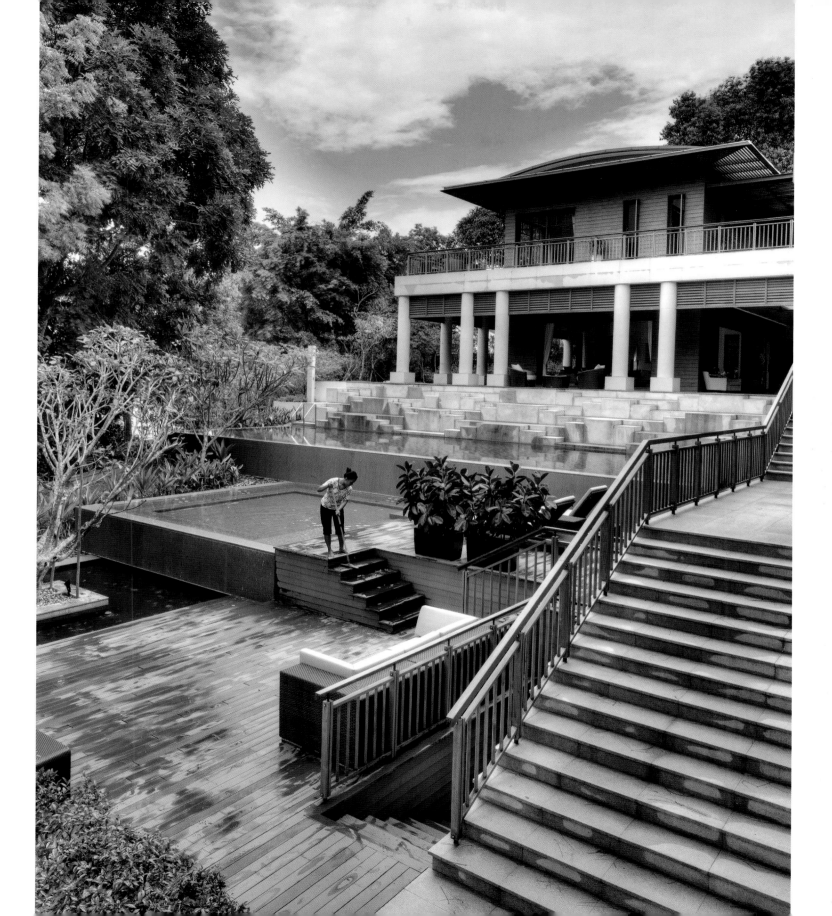

A HOUSE IN THREE MOVEMENTS
SINGAPORE
RT+Q ARCHITECTS

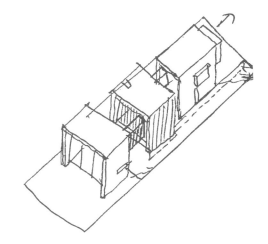

'The house is inspired by music composition. For instance, the composition of the house is divided into three movements, much like a symphony or a sonata. And in order to create a coherent overall composition, a leitmotif, in this case, three recurring spiral staircases, was invented and worked into the spaces of the house.'—Rene Tan

The architect, Rene Tan, was originally trained as a musician, so the musical metaphor should not be surprising. And the metaphor is worth analysing because it tells us a lot about how the house works. First, the movements of a piece of music are each separate and self-contained sections, but put together they form a unified whole. Secondly, a piece of music is also a work of art. Both points are crucial to how this house works, not just as some formal or intellectual idea but as a contemporary tropical house for a family.

The design team who worked with Rene Tan to achieve the success of the house included T. K. Quek, Chua Z. Chain, Joanne Goh and Jesslyn Ang.

The existing house on this narrow site had been semi-detached, but a bold decision was taken to set the new house back on both sides. This made the house even narrower than before, but opened up opportunities to draw far more light and air into it. The way this was done was to divide the house into three connected pavilions with each pavilion serving a distinct function. Hence, the front pavilion contains the public spaces—entry and living area on the first floor, a family and music room on the second floor and a roof terrace above. The second pavilion has an audio-visual room and maid's quarters in the basement, the kitchen and dining room on the first floor and the daughters' bedrooms, with a loft play space, on the second floor. The third pavilion has a guest bedroom and study on the first floor and the master bedroom with a grand walk-in wardrobe on the second floor.

These three pavilions are each given their own character by the materials used—timber cladding for the first, smooth white plaster for the second

and a rough-textured, striated grey concrete finish for the third. The three pavilions are joined by glass bridges and linked through courtyards which serve to separate each pavilion but also maintain visual connection because of the extensive glazing. Then there are the spiral staircases, what Tan calls the leitmotif, weaving its way through the music, an idea which is repeated, but in a slightly different form each time. The pivot to the house is the central staircase that spirals dynamically up from the basement through to the second level. A more delicate iron staircase winds its way up past the green wall in the courtyard off the family/music room to the roof terrace. Then a timber and steel staircase, with open risers, works its way up from the study to the walk-in wardrobe above.

The result of all this is a house of many parts, but all together forming a unity. This is achieved by glazing, including the transparent glass bridges, and by visual connection where from any one space other spaces can be glimpsed. It also means that

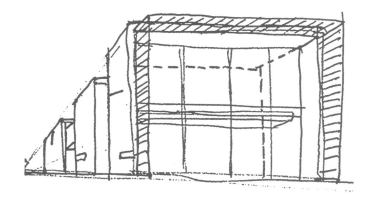

the house demonstrates another take on the issue of privacy and community. While there are many opportunities for the residents to be private, there is always a sense, because of all the connectivity, that they are together as a family.

A home, like a relationship, is a refuge. It is a place we return to for security, reassurance and endorsement. But, like a relationship, it should also offer the prospect of renewal. It is nice to be at home, to feel at home, to be somewhere familiar. But we also need to be regularly refreshed and have our perceptions regularly sharpened and reawakened. We need to be taken out of our complacency, away from the taken-for-granted.

This house offers many prospects, but they are all fugitive and ambiguous. Because of the transparency, we see a number of internal vistas layered over one another. We see the orthogonal structure of the house up against the curvilinear staircases. We see reflections in the glass and in mirrors. When we walk across the glass bridges, we have that fleeting moment of uncertainty as we look down through the glass to a lower level.

It is in these ways that the house becomes a work of art, heightening our awareness of where we are, why we are here and what we are doing here.

While this is most definitely a sustainable house in respect of its natural light, its cross-ventilation and its use of greenery and water to help cool the house, it is, like a work of art, emotionally and socially sustaining in the way it is constantly heightening awareness and refreshing the perceptions. It sustains a family by providing both private and communal amenity, but also by constantly reminding the residents of the value of what they have.

Opposite above left The music room on the second level of the front pavilion with a nicely edited view of the street.

Opposite above right The sitting room off the entry to the ground floor front pavilion.

Left The dining room in the middle pavilion, which leads directly off the front sitting room, has a certain informality to it with its banquette, breakfast bar and direct connection to the outside terrace and pool.

Right Looking back to the rear pavilion.

Above The master bedroom looks on to an atrium space. Elegant dark-stained joinery separates it from the walk-in wardrobe behind.

Left A spiral staircase links the walk-in wardrobe to the home office downstairs.

Opposite left The ground floor plan shows the three separate but linked pavilions.

Opposite centre The linking side corridor upstairs with its operable timber louvres.

Opposite above right The master bathroom in the third pavilion.

Opposite centre right The master bedroom.

Opposite bottom right The powder room in the ground floor entry pavilion.

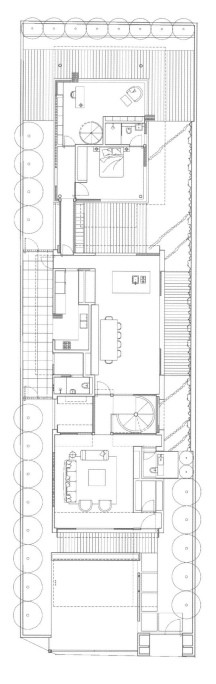

THE WINGED HOUSE
SINGAPORE
K2LD

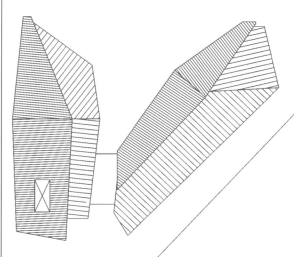

'Materiality is the key to strengthening the relationship of the two winged forms, its space in between and the roof-on-roof.'—Ko Shiou Hee

This challenging site was read as an opportunity by architect Ko Shiou Hee. The Winged House emerges from the ground as a simultaneously abstract and material expression of its place, celebrating its tropical context while at the same time indulging in a virtuosic play with form. The house is situated at the end of a cul-de-sac on a triangulated plot with a relatively steep slope leading down to a storm water canal. The triangular site and a stand of three mature palm trees at its lower edge gave the architect his inspiration.

Approaching the house, one meets two grand timber doors with vertical timber-framed slot windows on either side and above the transom. Open the doors and the eye is drawn immediately to the garden beyond and the three palm trees.

Where is the house? Well, it consists of two splayed volumes—two trapeziums—which pivot out from the central living space leading directly on from the entry doors. From the street, the house presents a mixed of dense materiality and transparency, with white render, timber screening

Above left Concept drawings of the roof forms.

Left The monolithic stone-walled entry is complemented by the soaring roof that appears to take flight.

Above When the entry door is open, the visitor sees straight through to the garden beyond.

Right The floating roof extends out to provide a canopy for the outdoor entertainment terrace.

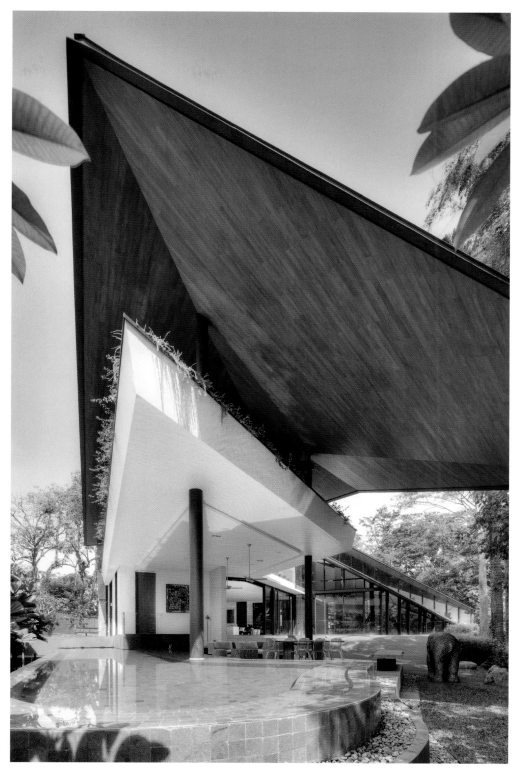

and two robust split granite walls on either side of the entry and extending inside the house. Once inside, the house opens up entirely to the lush tropical garden at the rear with the two trapezoidal forms framing the garden into a private, yet expansive, place for relaxing and entertaining. Framed by the thrusting roof forms, with the elevated living space looking down on the open tropical entertainment pavilion next to the swimming pool, the garden takes on the character of an open-air theatre.

In many ways, this is a house designed for gatherings and entertainment. The ground floor is the public realm. The kitchen and double-height dining room, entirely glazed on the garden side, are off to the left of the entry, while to the right the circulation leads the visitor out to the terrace and down the steps to the open entertainment pavilion and pool. The main guest bedroom is also down this side and has its own access to the pool. Also to the right of the entry are the stairs to the upper level where the master bedroom is linked by an open bridge-like corridor to two more bedrooms and a home office, which extends out to a timber deck framed and shaded by the plunging roof canopy. There is also a basement with an exercise room-cum-dance studio and a delightfully private parents' bedroom looking out to a garden lightwell and with one of the more opulent bathrooms you are ever likely to see. Its organic, cavernous, mosaic-tiled shower recess is an adventure in itself.

The architect speaks of the house in terms of two winged forms. This is because he has taken the two trapezoidal volumes and exploded them into a sculptural canopy that suggests a series of film frames of a bird's wings as it takes flight. The roof offers generous overhangs, providing shade and shelter from heavy rain. But it is a roof where roof is separated from roof, a dynamic interplay of

Right The living area is the pivot of the house, with the dining area angled off to the left and guest bedrooms to the right.

Below The lush garden is mirrored in the garden beds flanking the upper level of the house.

overlapping roofs. This opening up of the roof creates a play of light and shadow inside the house that is sustained at night by concealed lighting to illuminate the roof separation. Crucially, though, the separation of the roof enables a high degree of natural ventilation, allowing the house to largely forego air-conditioning.

The interplay of light and form is mirrored by the interplay of materials and by the way the house mixes materiality with transparency, as in the way the powerful split granite walls are juxtaposed to the glazing. The granite walls extend to the inside of the house where they contrast not just with the transparency to the garden but also with the delicate timber detailing and soaring ceilings. The use of timber itself offers further contrasts, as between the lighter-coloured Burmese teak for the underside of the roofs and the darker *chengai* as the infill medium used for the timber sunscreens.

The material selection and internal verticality of the house work together with the transparency to connect the house to its landscape context and its curtilage of tall trees. This connectivity is replicated in the programme of the house, which manages to blend the public and the private without any loss of privacy or any compromise to the theatricality of its public domain.

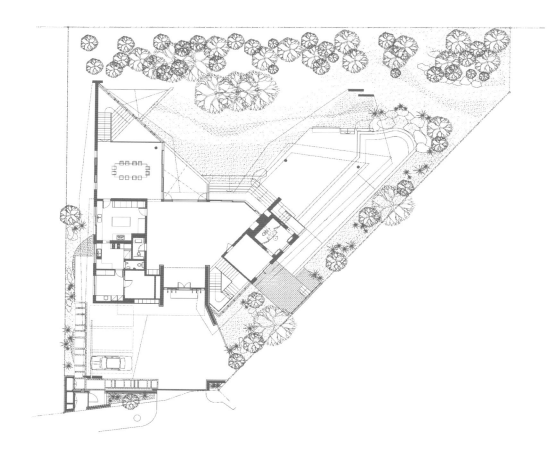

Far left The home office extends to an outside sitting area protected by the roof canopy.

Left The corridor linking the upstairs guest bedroom and the home office also serves as the library.

Right The parents' opulent bathroom where the shower recess is a glittering grotto.

Far right The stairs down from the dining area to the gym and parents' accommodation.

Below left The ground floor plan shows how the house is splayed into two pavilions pivoting around the living area.

Below The three existing palm trees which were the starting point for the plan.

CAIRNHILL SHOPHOUSE
SINGAPORE
RICHARD HO ARCHITECTS

Above The living area is part of one continuous space culminating in the dry kitchen and breakfast bar.

Left Garage and entry gate.

Opposite above The house is elevated above the road, allowing for a garage whose roof has been transformed into a terrace garden.

Right The house entry with the original casement windows now enlarged as French windows on to the terrace.

'The client specifically asked for a contemporary feel to the house. I believe we managed his expectations rather well. This house has all the trappings of modern comfort, yet it is unmistakably a shophouse which celebrates its heritage.'—Richard Ho

Richard Ho has a well-earned reputation for his sensitive but innovative work with conservation houses in Singapore and Malaysia. This reflects his strong commitment to cultural continuity. For Ho, this commitment is not some sentimental attachment to the past, but a vision of how the past can be constantly refreshed to inform a contemporary way of life. This is a form of cultural sustainability. In finding new uses for existing buildings, Ho is also contributing to environmental sustainability by minimizing waste and by employing climate control strategies to reduce energy consumption.

Ho's philosophy of a 'living past' is perfectly illustrated by his make-over of this pre-war terrace house on Cairnhill Road, just a short walk from bustling Orchard Road. The aim was to create a functional, contemporary family home while celebrating the house's history and character.

The façade was retained and restored, as were the internal party walls. A third level was added, but the necessary additional load-bearing columns and beams have been ingeniously disguised while attention is subtly drawn to the party walls and the airwell which are features of the shophouse/ terrace house. The original timber ceilings and flooring, along with the exposed beams, have also been retained, along with the tiling on the entry level terrace where the original casement windows have been elegantly enlarged to form French windows connecting the living area with the terrace.

The interior of the traditional shophouse can be dark, somewhat claustrophobic and spatially not suited to a contemporary lifestyle. Ho thus opened up the first floor into a single flowing space organized around the airwell. However, the original plan is very subtly retained. The living and dining areas form a single space, but the airwell now has a *koi* pond at its base, spanned by a timber bridge connecting with an eat-in dry kitchen and the wet kitchen, laundry and maid's quarters at the back.

With a timber-treaded stairway winding its way to the two upper levels, the airwell, described by Ho as the 'fulcrum of the house', becomes an atrium. No longer permanently open to the sky, the airwell has a retractable glass roof and operable blinds. Hence, it can be either open or closed depending on the weather, while the blinds reflect 75 per cent of the sun's heat back out. The climate control role of the traditional airwell has now been enhanced to be a source of natural light, a generator of natural ventilation and a means of heat control.

The airwell strategy, with its glass balustraded staircase, also creates a great sense of connectivity and transparency and the feeling that the house is unfolding vertically. As a result, the house has been opened up both in plan and verticality, eliminating the closed-in mood of the original shophouse.

In the Cairnhill Shophouse, Ho once again explores the Wrightian strategy of refuge and prospect. On the one hand, this is the perfect house for a young urban family because it is close to all the activity of the city. But once inside, it provides a sense of refuge from all the hustle and bustle outside. Inside, however, it offers expansive internal prospect. The stairway creates two 'wings' to the house—one, on the street side, a children's wing,

Above The master bathroom connects directly to the master bedroom.

Right By switching the stairway across a landing, the stairway becomes the 'fulcrum' of the house, leading the eye ever upwards.

the other, on the hill side, for parents and guests—visually connected across the airwell and through the glazed stairway balustrade.

The house backs on to a wooded hill, which not only provides privacy but the feeling that one is in the countryside, not in the middle of the Singapore CBD. Ho has 'borrowed' this landscape to achieve external prospect, in other words, a sense of connection with the natural world and an antidote to the feeling of enclosure that inevitably comes with a terrace house.

In the master bedroom, for example, customized joinery acts as a room divider and a bedhead, allowing the occupants to enjoy views through the bathroom to the landscape beyond, framed by a floor-to-ceiling window. Effectively, one is sleeping in the landscape, but without any loss of privacy. Then, on the top floor, Ho has created a timber-decked roof terrace with a plunge pool. The blade walls guarantee privacy as well as frame the landscape of the hill.

While this house offers refuge and prospect, it also offers privacy and community by providing communal spaces that are clearly separated from the private spaces, which include not just the children's wing but a beautifully appointed guest suite on the third storey reminiscent of a European roof space atelier.

Above The guest bedroom has its own special intimacy and privacy.

Right The rooftop deck and pool 'borrow' the landscape of the hill opposite.

Below The master bedroom is separated from the main volume of the house by a customized dividing wall.

COVE GROVE HOUSE 1
SENTOSA, SINGAPORE
AAMER ARCHITECTS

Right The splayed form of the building enables views and light to all parts of the house, reaching a climax with the glazed cube of the master bedroom.

Opposite below The ground floor plan and site plan show how the house optimizes its use of space and access to light and views.

Below The bold curvilinear form is signalled from the street, while the mass of the building is broken when the front door is opened, drawing the eye through to the other side.

'In some ways, our house represents who we are because we shape it. In other ways, it hints at who we will be because it shapes us.'—Owner

The clients for this house speak of their awareness of the 'two-way interactions between the environment and our inner selves', which they say has been generated by having lived in many places around the world, including the US, UK, Malaysia, Hong Kong and China. It is not surprising then that they were not looking for a fashion statement when they commissioned Aamer Taher to design their new house—a *home* with all that the word implies.

Those implications are reflected in most of the houses in this book. For example, there is the Frank Lloyd Wright notion of refuge and prospect. In this case, however, the house is not so much a refuge because the clients work from home and do not need to flee the city rat race. On the other hand, Sentosa Island is rapidly becoming a byword for overdevelopment and vulgar architecture, albeit with some notable exceptions. Thus, the clients were looking to block out as much of the Sentosa housing as possible while still taking advantage of the better views, principally of the waterways at the front and back.

Aamer Taher has obliged by designing a building which has what he calls a 'boomerang' shape. The site is long and narrow with a small water frontage. The curved shape enables all the bedrooms to have views of the water and has allowed a 25-metre swimming pool which extends around the fully glazed living/dining pavilion to become a water feature in itself, including a small island with a tree whose form is mirrored in the columns that support

the cantilevered cube of the master bedroom. The living/dining pavilion is connected by a timber bridge over the lawn to the waterfront pier. This bridge is continued as a deck down the side of the pavilion and together they give the impression that the pavilion is floating on water.

The fluid form of the house gives the building a distinctive character in the context of the rectilinear enfilade of the other houses along the waterfront. It also feels bigger and creates a sense of freedom that would have been hard to achieve had it conformed to the typical grid.

The two-way external prospect is revealed immediately the front door is opened, because the free-flowing spaces enable a through view from the street to the water on the other side. These free-flowing spaces, along with the generous glazing on the rear elevation of the house, also create internal prospect as the eye is led easily from one space to another and, eventually, to the outside landscape and water views.

But the street elevation is more about refuge. At ground level it is a curving solid, stone-clad wall with only narrow vertical slot windows. The upper level is a solid plastered wall, this time with horizontal slot windows which peer out almost suspiciously to the street. The contrast of the dark stone-clad lower façade with the white upper façade—like the rear elevation—serves to 'dematerialize' the building, break down its mass and create the sense that the building is floating.

In section, the house emphasizes the distinction between the private and communal domains. Where the ground level spaces flow effortlessly into one

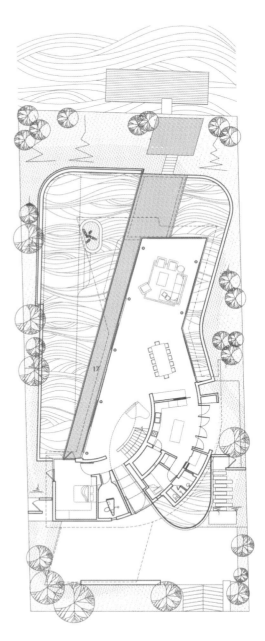

another, from the entry space with its kitchen and breakfast area to the expansive living/dining space with baby grand piano, the upper level is more compartmentalized. Here, the master bedroom is separated from the guest and future children's bedrooms by an open entertainment pod. This second storey has a certain mystery to it since curving corridors ensure privacy between spaces, even offering a little outside terrace for quiet reflection or a read.

The clients, a professional couple who invest in the global market, work from home in order to operate more easily across different world time zones. This means that the house has a third domain—a fully equipped home office on the third storey of the house.

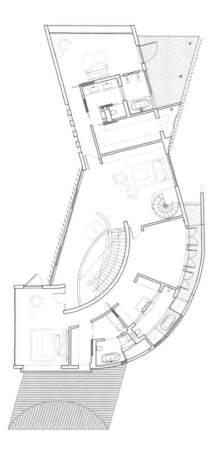

Above Second storey floor plan.

Right The stairway and its glass balustrading continue the curvilinear theme.

Above left All-round glazing dematerializes the ground floor spaces to unify the interior with the exterior garden and pool.

Left The Japanese stone garden on the roof provides the opportunity for restorative breaks from the home office.

This is effectively a glazed pavilion on the top of the house consisting of a library/sitting area which steps up to the office space. This space is divided into two offices—one for each of them—but is visually connected by a glass wall. This mezzanine is open to the library but is physically defined by a day bed, presumably providing the means for a little reflection on investment strategy or a nap between time zones.

A different kind of refuge and prospect is offered by the roof of the house in the form of a Japanese stone garden which runs from the home office to the front, providing a space for relaxation and meditation, along with some stunning views.

The house is thus divided into three domains—social, family and work. As the clients say, 'These are three different yet intertwined aspects of modern life. We strive to achieve a harmonious balance of these three elements in our house.'

The decision to adopt a curvilinear principle as the design driver for the house has resulted in a distinctive unity. The external curved form is mirrored on the inside by the free-flowing spaces downstairs, the dramatic curved staircase to the second storey, culminating in a curved balustrade which both defines another sitting area and signals the start of the journey to the guest rooms, the stairway to the rooftop home office and, finally, the stone garden.

It is a design concept which sustains a unique way of life both in terms of how people live inside the house and in terms of how the house responds to its context—basically by turning its back on the urban context but embracing the context of the natural world.

Left Looking back from the living area to the dining area, music room and stairway leading to the second level.

Above The master bedroom enjoys its own private deck.

Right A small sitting area at the top of the stairs.

Below The curved wall on one side enlivens the sitting area so that it is much more than a glass viewing box.

Top The library offers a quiet reading space away from the rest of the house.

Top right A sitting area on the second level with the spiral staircase to the home office in the background.

Above Part of the home office on the roof of the house has views back into Sentosa and a canal.

Right Looking back from the water, it is possible to appreciate the dynamic splayed, thrusting form of the building and the way it opens itself up to its location.

COVE GROVE HOUSE 2
SINGAPORE
BEDMAR & SHI

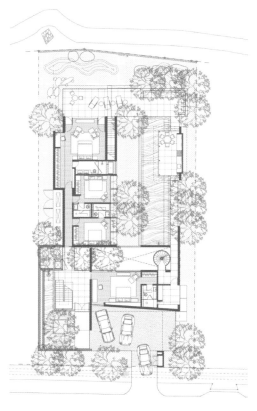

'This house is designed to make full use of the view. We wanted every room to enjoy the view while remaining private.'—Ernesto Bedmar

On Sentosa Island there are views—and there are views. This house has *the* view, out to the ocean and several small islands and enlivened by the off-centre flotilla of moored ships and the constant to and fro of smaller vessels.

Cove Grove House 2 is a typical Ernesto Bedmar house in that it gives little away from the street, quietly insisting on its privacy and turning its back on the road in order to open up to the sea at the rear. Entry to the house is via stepping stones 'floating' over a pond which extends down the side of the entry vestibule. Once inside, the visitor faces a glass-enclosed void with a tree growing up from the basement level. The choice then is either to proceed directly ahead down a corridor leading past two guest bedrooms to the master bedroom, to turn right into the main guest bedroom, or to go up a folded staircase to the upper level.

Led by the light in the double-height glass vestibule, the choice is to ascend the stairs. At the top, it becomes clear that this is an L-shaped building embracing a tropical garden and a swimming pool with a gazebo. Once again, we can turn right, this time into the dining room and kitchen, or proceed straight ahead down a corridor lined on the left by timber shelving with a variety of traditional artefacts lit by inset LED lights.

Now the whole purpose of the house is revealed as we enter a splendid living pavilion leading directly to a 4.5-metre cantilevered deck and panoramic ocean views. The deck extends the full width of the

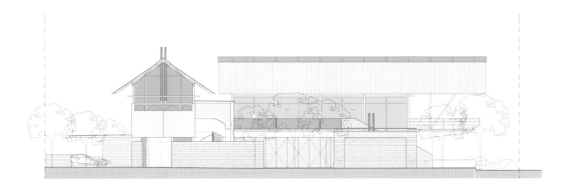

Opposite above Seen from the waterfront, the house sits behind a fence of wooden bollards, with the eye drawn to its tropical roof form.

Opposite below Ground floor plan.

Left The long elevation shows how the guest and dining pavilion is almost independent of the main house.

Below The timber-framed gazebo by the pool responds to the enfilade of timber screens masking the bedrooms.

Above A mezzanine entertainment space sits above the living area.

Right The theme of refined timber detailing is announced at the street entry of the house which, typically, gives little away.

Opposite above The living area enjoys a tropical high-pitched timber roof cooled by Boffi fans, with a dynamic circular staircase going up to the entertainment room.

Opposite below The entry vestibule is a transitional space with a ceremonial feel.

THE SUSTAINABLE ASIAN HOUSE

house and is covered to provide protection from the western sun. Inside, the living room is a fine example of Bedmar's signature tropical refinement. The ceiling is steeply pitched to emulate a typical tropical home. The frame is steel but the trusses are timber-clad to simulate a more traditional structure. At the apex is a triangulated skylight screened by timber battens. The high-pitched roof and the Boffi ceiling fans minimize the need for air-conditioning.

A spiral staircase leads up from the living area to a mezzanine, a more intimate sitting room with its own special framed view out to the sea.

Flooring throughout the house is Canadian brushed oak, which contrasts with the use of teak for the exterior cladding and the vertical batten screens that provide privacy down the northern side of the house which has some exposure to the neighbours. The use of timber is counterpointed

Above The entertainment space sits under the pitched roof.

Right The guest bedroom, which is immediately off the entry, enjoys total privacy.

against the use of a neutral beige limestone and a dark grey polished granite floor at the downstairs entry. The only departure from the refined tropical finishes are the customized rough-hewn timber tables from Bali in the living room and the long table in the dining room.

Downstairs, the corridor acts as a spine, with two guest bedrooms off to the side, culminating in the master bedroom which looks straight out through a feature window to the sea. But the setback of 6.5 metres, along with a small grassy berm separated from the public walkway by timber bollards, ensures complete privacy. A combination of cantilevered deck and external screens means the ground level remains shaded and cool.

Upstairs, the corridor opens on to a small television sitting room separated from the main living room by a timber cube containing a powder room. Once again, the deck with its timber canopy modulates the light, provides protection from the sun and captures the sea breeze, making the use of air-conditioning rarely necessary.

The modulation of light throughout the house is an aspect of the way Bedmar has been able to provide privacy while still engaging with the view. The main guest bedroom is an excellent example. On the ground floor, it forms the foot of the L shape. Right by the entry, it is quite separate from the rest of the house and enjoys a sublimely intimate view out to the garden, past the pool and out to an edited view of the sea. Directly above it, the dining room is more light-filled and offers a more expansive view of the water as well as views down into the garden and pool.

The house is for a single man who uses it as a weekend retreat and for entertaining friends. This is just as well because, if one lived here permanently, one would never want to leave. It is a beautiful balance of intimacy and openness. The views range from the grand seascape to private garden nooks. It also offers a variety of spatial experiences so that the house has many stories to tell. In addition, the house, like all Bedmar houses, has a powerful haptic or tactile quality due to the finishes, the subtle decorative touches and the rhythmic organization of the spaces. In short, Cove Grove 2 House is an emotionally and socially sustaining house whose ample natural light and ventilation also lend it strong environmental credentials.

THE PARTY HOUSE
SINGAPORE
W ARCHITECTS

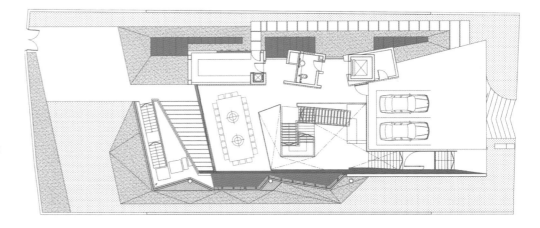

'The ritual is that you enter, have a drink, then progress to dinner upstairs. It is really a series of coloured boxes and each room is treated like a little jewel.'—Mok Wei Wei

Describing this house with its opulent finishes as 'sustainable' might be just a touch tongue in cheek, but only a touch because there is a serious side to this house, built mainly for having parties. After all, what is a party if not something designed to sustain a social network, relationships and friendships? Many houses devote part of their plan to enter-taining family and friends but this one devotes itself entirely to this agenda.

Relationships, whether between family members or between friends, invariably have a ritual element to them. In fact, the ritual is crucial to sustaining those relationships. We meet at certain times and in the same place, we do the same things, eat the same food, and do everything according to a set and mutually agreed routine or order. By observing the ritual, we are silently reassuring one another that our relationship is still alive and well.

This house on Singapore's Sentosa Island is designed to embody, indeed express, that ritual. It consists of a basement area, two levels above, along with what the architect calls an 'attic'—a box sitting on top of the main structure—with an adjacent rooftop deck and swimming pool. As the architect comments, 'the design creates a sequence of spaces to form a unique stage for entertainment'.

There is a ritual progression in the experience of the house. This begins by walking down a slope to the basement for pre-dinner drinks. This room is a shell of off-form concrete defined by pools of light and a soaring double-height void containing the dining area, effectively a mezzanine, linked to the basement by a grand stairway. The basement is like a cavern, a kind of moody, underlit domestic night-club. Down one side is a long glass wall, behind which is a tropical garden with a green wall and a pond. This garden extends to the outside of the house on the southern or sea side, becoming a double-height green wall. The basement also con-tains two bedrooms, one enjoying a dry pebble garden courtyard at the bottom of a lightwell.

After drinks, the guests proceed to the dining area with its long dining table lit by the extravagant Karim Rashid 'Topography' chandelier. This space, which is at ground level, looks out to sea with a

small berm serving to block out the public walkway in front and create the illusion that the view belongs exclusively to this house. On this level and above, the robust off-form concrete is replaced by polished black granite flooring and black metal ceilings.

After dinner, guests make their way up to the second level where there are three entertainment rooms clustered around a long, illuminated onyx bar. Each room is a glowing glass box with its own

Top The upper level of the house can be screened off by an aluminium chain curtain.

Above Plan showing the basement level and mezzanine floor.

Right At night, with the aluminium curtain open, the internal glazed rooms gleam like lanterns.

Right The section reveals how guests move through the house as on a journey.

Far right Looking up from the basement entry, guests can immediately see the vertical progression of spaces and how the evening will unfold.

Left The women's after dinner room is a white lantern with sunken seating.

Below Guests enter at basement level where the mood is more like a nightclub than a home.

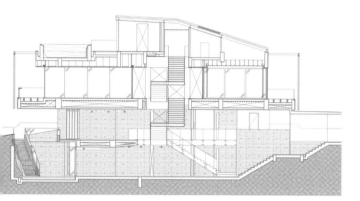

distinctive colour which is refracted after dark by the fretting covering the lower third of every wall. The 'Gentlemen's Club' is yellow, the 'Ladies' Winter Room' is white with a glowing drop ceiling made of glass, sunken seating and a fireplace, while the 'Karaoke Lounge' is a decadent purple. This level is completely surrounded by a wide verandah with a continuous aluminum chain curtain which eliminates the need for framing and which can be drawn or pulled aside to embrace the view. This verandah is accessed through glass doors where glass meets glass to create the illusion that there is no separation.

The attic space is the final stage of the ritual. It is a 'summer room', a broad pavilion-like space whose folding glass doors open on to the deck and the raised infinity-edge pool clad in glittering mosaic tiles. This, says the architect, 'connects the sky and the sea'. To sit here or lounge in the pool is to feel that it is just you and the view with the neighbours cropped out.

Here, the ritual reaches its apotheosis. From the moody, almost rugged 'lower depths', up through two refined, polished and richly coloured levels, the journey culminates in casting aside all sense of enclosure as one enjoys the marinescape on a balmy tropical night tempered by the sea breeze.

Left From the rooftop cabana, the horizon is illuminated by the lights of moored ships.

Right The long dining table on the mezzanine floor.

Below The men's after dinner room has the palette of a gentlemen's club.

Above Over the infinity edge of the pool, the lights of moored ships can be seen on the horizon.

Right The pool and cabana are set back from the front of the house to provide privacy from the public walkway below.

Below At night, from the public walkway along the waterfront, the house glows like a multicoloured lantern.

INDONESIA

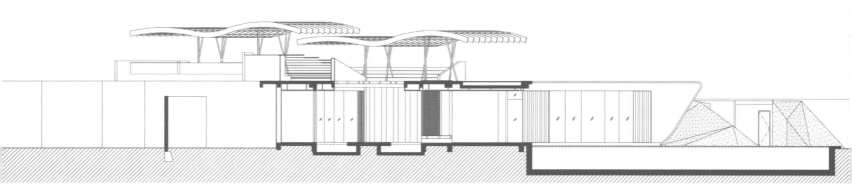

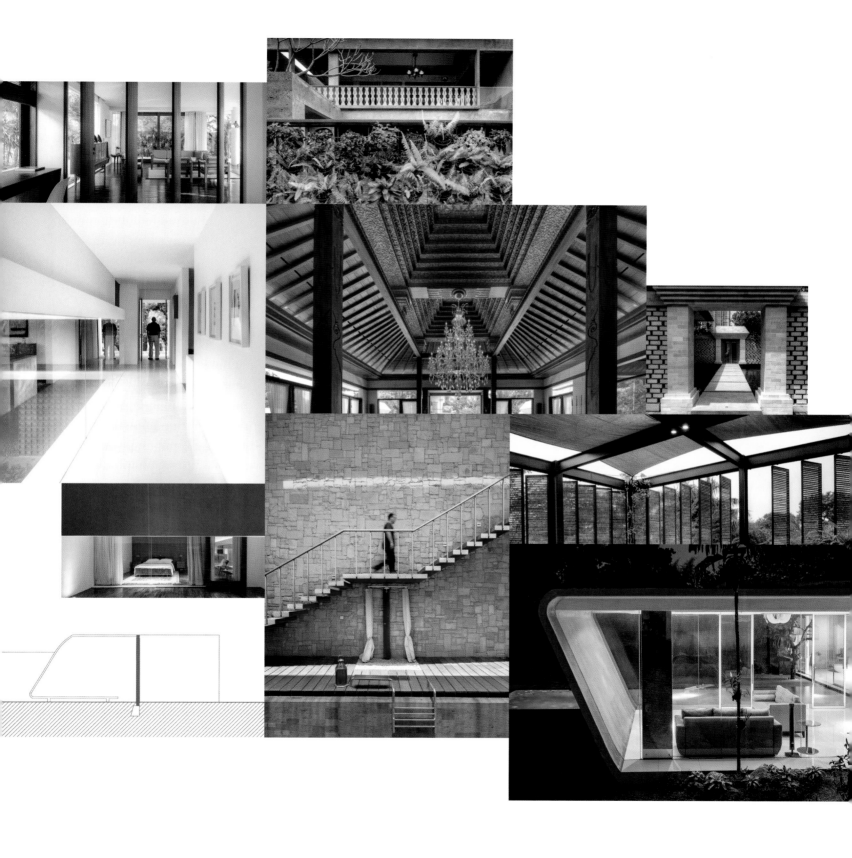

BRAWIJAYA HOUSE
JAKARTA, INDONESIA
HAN AWAL ARCHITECTS

Left Looking towards the small traditional gate that leads guests through garden courts to the outdoor entertainment area at the rear of the house.

Right The poolside cabana at the back of the house continues the theme of traditional building types.

Below The double-height outdoor entertainment area viewed from the cabana.

'For me, the outcome of this house was different from other houses I have worked on. Yori and his client gave soul to the house. I pulled the concept together from the architect, the client and the craftsmen.'—Rudi Dodo, interior designer

Architect Yori Antar has a passionate commitment to sustaining traditional Indonesian arts and crafts, including traditional building practices. He has initiated and documented projects on Flores, Sumba and Nias, helping villagers to build new homes employing traditional techniques.

With the Brawijaya House, he was able to pursue his agenda of cultural sustainability in an urban context because his client was equally passionate about sustaining a living culture, especially Javanese dance. Indeed, one enters the house through a recreated traditional *pendopo* or reception hall, which the client uses for dance performances.

The owner had requested a house inspired by the Javanese *kraton* style, that is, the traditional house or palace of the sultan. Yori Antar's response was to design the house in a blend of the traditional and the modern. Walking through the Brawijaya House from the entry to the rear pool and the garden, the experience is indeed one of fluid transition from the traditional to the modern.

Surrounded by a high wall, the house is not very visible from the street. Once inside, however, it is apparent that the house occupies most of the plot. There are two entries. From the *porte cochère* there is a small traditional gate leading to a lovely extended garden down the side of the house, which acts as a kind of public arrival route leading to the swimming pool, cabana and entertainment deck. From the pool garden it is possible to see how the architectural form of the house echoes traditional practice, in particular the high-pitched roof (*joglo*) and the deeply recessed verandahs.

The main entry to the house is through imposing double timber doors carved by the Balinese wood sculptor Made Sudiana, whose wife is Javanese and whose work shows a strong Javanese influence.

These doors are an early signal that the house will reflect the highly eclectic nature of Javanese culture, which has been influenced over the centuries by China and India via the trade routes, by the arrival of Islam and by the Dutch and British colonialists. The cultural mix is expressed in the architecture through high-pitched roofs, deeply recessed verandahs and covered linked walkways through tropical gardens, while the interiors feature traditional timber carving and an eclectic mix of Javanese and colonial antiques.

Once inside, the first space is the *pendopo* with its traditional high-pitched roof and exposed central square-framed truss supporting the upper roof. The high roof volume and central, customized terracotta tiles from Jogjakarta, designed by Rudi Dodo and based on traditional motifs, are natural cooling elements. A traditional chandelier throws light up to the carved timber ceiling to create a play of shadows, while the space is decorated with a variety

Above The main living area is a mix of the old and the new. A central galleria leads to the dining room while side doors lead to contrasting courtyards.

Left The dining room, which transitions from the traditional *gebyok* walls and screen doors across to the contemporary tropical water garden.

Right The *pendopo* celebrates traditional Javanese craft and is a room dedicated to dance performances.

Right The water garden off the dining room.

Far right above Detail of the carved timber entry doors by Made Sudiana.

Far right below A galleria links the *pendopo* and the living space with a side entry into the dining room.

of antique pieces, such as a large colonial mirror and cabinets and a *tombak* or Javanese spear stand.

The next space is the dining room, a long room which literally transitions from old to modern from one side of the room to the other. Here we find the *pièce de résistance* of the whole house, the recreated *gebyok* or traditional Javanese wall. Originally four-sided, this extraordinarily intricate, hand-carved feature is effectively two-sided, with mirrors and internal lighting used to simulate the four sides. A three-generation company of craftsmen was employed to carve the wall and doors, based on initial designs by Rudi Dodo, which open out on to a spacious terrace and garden. On the other side of the dining table, which is carved from a single piece of teak, the space becomes modern with a white stone wall and folding glass doors leading to a water garden with a black granite ziggurat-shaped fountain designed by Yori Antar.

From the dining room one moves into the living room, with the master bedroom off to the right. It is a further progression from the old to the new, an essentially modern room but decorated with antiques sourced from Kota Gede, near Jogjakarta. The progression culminates in a double-height terrace looking on to the swimming pool and across to the cabana, a perfectly symmetrical example of tropical modern.

The Brawijaya House successfully maintains cultural continuity while making a major statement about how traditional crafts can be sustained through contemporary application. It is also an excellent demonstration of how traditional architectural practice—for example, the deep verandahs which effectively create garden rooms—can naturally cool the house and provide a tropical oasis in the middle of a busy city.

Top The luxuriant pool garden has the feel of a tropical resort.

Above The entry to the poolside cabana with its stone structure hints at a bathing ritual.

SENJAYA HOUSE
JAKARTA, INDONESIA
RT+Q ARCHITECTS

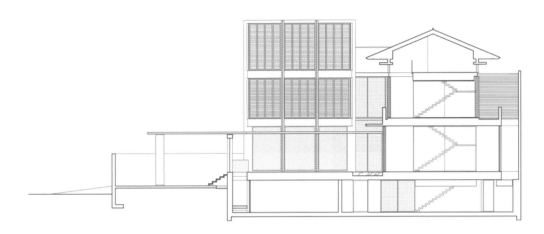

There is nothing more sustaining than an oasis. This house is an oasis in the middle of hectic, noisy Jakarta, defined by a necklace of filigreed *bushida* trees whose delicate tracery helps screen the house from the street while shading the high protective wall and the gardens within.

Like any oasis, there is an outer screen and an inner domain with this house, a world within a world. In this case, after entering from the *porte cochère* through a timber door set in a rough-hewn

Above The section shows how the timber-screened box appears to float almost independently of the rest of the house.

Below The *porte cochère* where the Craggy Lava stone wall and looming 'keep' immediately create a sense of entering a castle.

Opposite The castle 'keep' floats mysteriously above the fully transparent living room and timber-decked pool.

local Craggy Lava stone feature wall, there is a tranquil garden courtyard with a *koi* pond at the far end. The house wraps itself around this green-grassed central space in a U shape. On all three sides of this embrace there is total transparency as the house opens itself up to the cool central court. On one side, there is the living pavilion, separated from the main house by a breezeway. This pavilion is thoroughly transparent, both from the internal garden court and to the deck and pool on the other side. Opposite the living pavilion is the pantry, a word that hardly describes this light-filled and expansive breakfast room which is set, somewhat theatrically, on a raised podium and reached by walking up a low set of steps. This gives the pavilion a temple-like feel, which in turn transforms the garden court into a kind of forecourt, a transitional space leading to the crucial inner sanctum.

All of this suggests another analogy at work—the subtle hint of a Japanese castle. From the street, what catches the eye is the soaring triple-storey timber-screened tower above the living pavilion. In terms of the castle analogy, this is the tower or keep (*tenshu*). Like any castle, there are spaces within spaces. Hence, at the entry off the street there is a massive stone wall (*uchikomihagi*), the equivalent

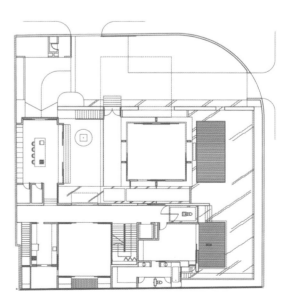

THE SUSTAINABLE ASIAN HOUSE

Left Looking from the living room to the floating poolside deck.

Opposite below left The elevated pantry, an elegant modernist glass pavilion, is across a grassy courtyard from the living room.

Opposite below right The ground floor plan illustrates the sense of entering a castle courtyard.

Below The upstairs living/entertainment room has its own external courtyard.

of the base of the temple. What follows is a progression into the internal garden court, with the ceremonial steps up to the breakfast room and a view up to the elegant, dark-stained timber keep, its horizontal timber louvres screening the master bedroom and the roof terrace above it. Now the house conjures up images of the floating Japanese castles known as *ukishiro*, built on flat land and surrounded by water. On top of the tower, fittingly, the occupants can look out over the neighbourhood from an expansive, shaded rooftop sitting area. Effectively double-height, this is a space for relaxation and for enjoying barbeques. Sitting on top of the house, it captures any breeze that may be blowing, while the embracing timber louvred screens provide privacy and beautifully modulated

light, at the same time giving a sense of connection with the outside world.

Although the house transitions from public to increasingly private domains, there is a unifying transparency. The U shape is almost entirely glazed, and when the sliding glass doors on either side of the living pavilion are open, there is a continuous space from garden through living to timber poolside deck. Even inside the house, a single pivoting timber door accesses the powder room which, with its outer timber screen doors open, is in effect part of the pool. Likewise, the ground floor dining room off the crossbar of the U shape opens on to a small open-air court with another rough-hewn stone wall. Upstairs, on the crossbar, is a television room, again fully glazed, this time opening on to a timber deck.

The clients' brief to architect Rene Tan and his design team of T. K. Quek and Jonathan Quek had been simple: 'It should be a very relaxed house and generate air circulation.' In these ways, the architect and his team have delivered on the clients' requirements—a socially sustaining house with ample cross-ventilation and no great need for air-conditioning. This cross-ventilation, along with the use of timber screens, shading trees, grass courtyard and water, is highly effective in cooling the house. This is supported by the orientation of the house and a variety of interventions—trees, blank walls and blade walls—which minimize the house's exposure to direct sun.

Essentially, the house is a community of spaces, separate yet connected. For this reason, it is a house which sustains the community of the family, bringing everyone together yet still providing private space, for example, in the way the parents and children have their own wings. Complementing this social sustainability is the way in which the house is so effectively cooled and ventilated naturally.

Above The rooftop entertainment deck, with its operable timber louvred screens, gives the sense of living amongst the treetops.

Below The master bedroom sits in the lower level of the timber-screened box.

Below The master bathroom.

Above Looking back from the pantry across the courtyard to the living pavilion, its entry gate open.

Left The exquisite powder room-cum-breezeway has a direct link to the pool.

Right The floating pool deck, with the powder room to the left, is part of a serene tropical garden.

R HOUSE
JAKARTA, INDONESIA
BUDI PRADONO ARCHITECTS

Left The dynamic form of the living pavilion thrusts like a boat past the pool.

Right The fully transparent glass living pavilion.

Below The section shows canopies for the rooftop garden that have not been installed.

'The owner asked me, "Can you redefine my architectural identity? I want this to be a traditional house but in a modern way." Cohabitation is therefore the main theme—cohabitation with the community and with the family.'—Budi Pradono

The R House is located in a gated community, Tana Peru, at Depok on the fringes of Jakarta and near the University of Indonesia, hence home to many teachers from the university. This means that Tana Peru is not just defined by a surrounding fence but by common values. With this in mind, Budi Pradono wanted the house to be porous— connected to its context, allowing the outside in and revealing the inside to the outside. For Pradono, this context was not just social, but also natural. Hence, it is a house with a close connection to the outside landscape and the changing light of the day. Pradono retained as many of the existing trees as possible, including several inside the house and even some growing up through the roof.

Originally, the client wanted a renovation of an existing house, but with two growing children and two cars to accommodate, it quickly became clear that more space was needed. When the client revealed that he had acquired a considerable amount of land at the rear of the house, it was decided to rebuild and extend further back.

The house now sits above the street with a garage below street level. The organization of the house is a journey from the public domain through transitional spaces to the private domain, from the old to the new, from the traditional to the modern.

The steps up to the open verandah suggest a ritual of arrival. The verandah itself is a traditional gesture, a variation on Patawi buildings, Patawi being the local clan from which the client is descended. Open to the public domain, the house is intended to entertain neighbours and even features a traditional *bale* or raised platform for sleeping or sitting on and a central square of recycled Dutch-era floor tiles. There is also a *koi* pond, signalling the use of water as a unifying element throughout the house. The client is a keen diver, so the water is intended partly to reflect his character, as does the basic plan of making the house more fluid as it extends into the private realm.

On the verandah, patterned screens made from recycled timber offer views to the interior of the house and the next transitional space, thus emphasizing the porosity. This space has ramps down to the garage and service area as well as guest accommodation. Beyond this it steps up to an entry terrace and another pond before turning a corner to the concealed entry door.

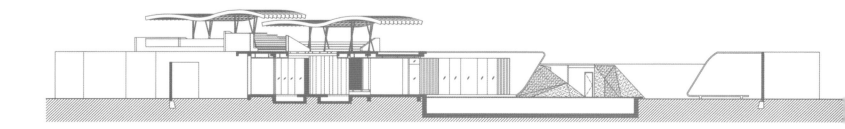

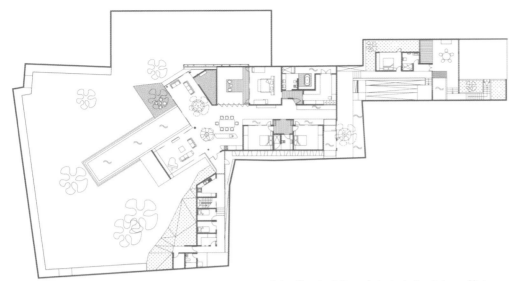

Once inside, the private domain comprises a straight spine with moats on either side. On the left is the children's wing, reached by a small wooden bridge and through a stone portal. On the right is the parent's wing, where the master bedroom looks out into a private court. This is visible from the spine through a timber screen, while there are views out to the rear garden through organically shaped windows. Between the master bedroom and the walk-in wardrobe is the master bathroom. Once again, there is a pond, with a free-standing bath sitting on a timber deck that 'floats' over the pond, allowing its bathers to enjoy the light and air of the open void.

At the end of the central spine is the dining area where the house opens up in three directions. To the right is an open space leading to the prayer room, which also serves as a study and discussion

Below The circulation culminates in the dining and living areas, with a sitting area to the right and two existing trees thrusting up through the ceiling.

Above Looking down the circulation spine towards the inside entry to the house, with moats on either side and the children's rooms to the right.

Below The house is a composition of thrusting transparent forms.

Above A small timber bridge signals the transition from the entry and guest area to the main part of the house.

area and acts, as far as the client is concerned, as the fulcrum to the house. Directly ahead is the living area while, to the left, is the pantry. This entire space comprises a light-filled garden pavilion that embraces the expansive rear garden area.

But the house has not yet exhausted its cohabitation possibilities because there is also a rooftop garden with a roof form providing what Pradono describes as 'a new public space' in the form of sitting areas.

In sum, this is a house which is culturally and socially sustainable, embracing its neighbours and employing traditional building styles and materials, including local stone, such as andrasit and porous mountain sandstone.

It is also an environmentally responsive house. The architectural plan ensures that the house is protected from direct sun, except for the morning sun on the rear of the house. It also generates plentiful natural ventilation. Only three rooms have air-conditioning and that is timed to operate only at night. Rain water is collected and used for the ponds, while the green grassed roof has a cooling effect on the house.

Above The elevated 'community' verandah at the entry, with the raised platform or *bale* for sleeping or sitting on.

Above right The walk-in wardrobe for the master bedroom.

Right The house entry, its vertical timber louvre screen creating a connection between the inside and outside.

Far left A view down to the pool area reveals how well the existing trees have been accommodated in the plan.

Above left The master bedroom enjoys its own private courtyard, with visual links to the internal corridor and to the garden.

Above all, the R House is an emotionally sustainable house—calm, quiet and reassuring, with the constant, soothing sound of running water. It also tracks the changing light of the day through the patterns of timber and perforated metal screens and skylights.

'I love to create an ambiguous space', says Pradono, 'which depends on the interpretation of people when they enter the space.'

RUMAH TINGGAL PRAJA
JAKARTA, INDONESIA
D-ASSOCIATES

Right The house seen from the street entry.

Below The internal courtyard looking towards the street, with the extruded horizontal timber screen shading the pool.

'For us, the context of the project was always the place, the site itself, which means you have the land, the climate, the existing location and the users as context.'—Gregorius Supie Yolodi

Rumah Tinggal Praja is located in a very old part of Jakarta, a tapestry of narrow streets just off a major thoroughfare. The clients did not want the house to stand out but to respect the scale and character of the neighbourhood. Indeed, it settles easily into its urban context—independent but not imposing. The house gives little away to the street, but equally it does not turn its back on the street which is surprisingly active with a variety of traffic, including food and drinks vendors. Its engagement with the outside is subtle. Its concrete façade is modulated by slots of colour-back glass and a screen across the upper level made of operable translucent glass louvres.

Above The entry vestibule provides a transition from the public to the private domains, its timber and stone surfaces providing a hint of what is to come.

Below The section reveals how the house has a ceremonial quality in the way the spaces open up sequentially.

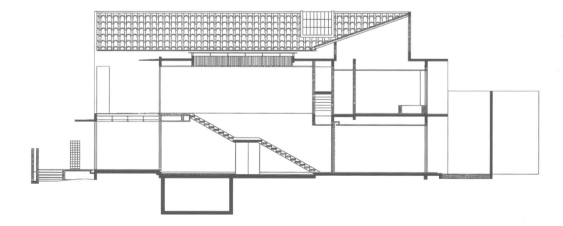

Once past the outside gate and wall, custom-designed double doors made of recycled timber admit the visitor to a vestibule clad in wood and stone, a transitional space from the public to the private realm. From here, guests pass into the private domain, organized around a double-height courtyard open to the sky with a swimming pool down the centre.

The house itself is L-shaped, with the public areas on the ground floor and the private quarters on the upper level. Down the left-hand side are guest amenities, a study and storage. A small garden courtyard separates this wing from the expansive living/dining/pantry space opposite the entry and opening out through two massive steel-framed glass doors to the rear garden whose privacy is guarded by a high wall.

Down the right-hand side of the central court is an imposing full-height, rough-hewn, randomly assembled Javanese sandstone feature wall. This wall separates the family home from the service areas, which are remarkably generous.

Far left The random sandstone wall forms an impressive backdrop to the pool and the grand stairway to the upper level.

Left This view down into the pool area and the living room shows the open roof.

Right A massive pivoting glass door off the dining area leads to the rear garden.

Below The fully glazed side wall and pivoting glass doors of the living room create a full connection with the shaded garden.

A timber stairway scales up alongside the wall to a bridge and the glass louvred screen already visible from the street. Down the left-hand side are the children's bedrooms and a study, separated again by the garden void before culminating in the master bedroom. In the corner, two recycled traditional Javanese timber doors give access to a rooftop garden.

In many ways, the house suggests the plan of a shophouse crossed, perhaps, with a Moorish courtyard house. Certainly, in its environmental characteristics it is close to those typologies. On the one hand, it is a series of spaces intersected by an airwell. On the other, it wraps itself around a central water garden with the upper galleries looking down into a court.

Architect Gregorius Supie Yolodi explains that the couple, who have one school-age daughter, 'like to be open, they don't like to show off'. They wanted space for living, says Supie, 'so this plan adapts to those issues.' Part of that adaptation is a high level of transparency and connectivity. Vertically and in plan, the house forms an organic unity.

Openness and transparency draw in so much natural light that electric light hardly ever has to be used during the day. Likewise, the cross-ventilation is such that the need for air-conditioning is minimal. In addition, when the sun hits the pool, it causes evaporation which is then fed through the house by the cross-ventilation, providing even more natural cooling. This is enhanced by other features. All the existing trees were retained, providing shade as well as a cooling effect. Timber venetian blinds, along with the timber slatted screen with the glass canopy partly extruding over the courtyard, cast intriguing shadow patterns and induce a sense of stillness and calm, which psychologically contributes to the cool atmosphere.

Above The privacy of the master bedroom, despite its fully glazed wall and connection to the garden, is guarded by the high party wall.

Above right The small side garden court forms a void linking the ground floor and upper level.

Right The master bedroom is shaded by a delicate timber louvre screen.

This house is a good neighbour, doing its bit to sustain an old and established community. Inside, it offers privacy from the outside world but also for the individual inhabitants, including the domestic staff. But this is not at the expense of internal community because of the close visual and physical connection between the interior spaces. The communal areas—around the pool and the large living space—are directly linked to the private quarters. In fact, the living space and its contiguous garden were deliberately planned to enable the residents to entertain large numbers of people, especially their church community. In short, this is a house with strong environmental, social and cultural sustainability credentials.

Right The recycled timber entry doors are flanked by delicate timber battened screens.

Opposite above right Ground floor plan.

Opposite below right The timber-screened vestibule from the car port.

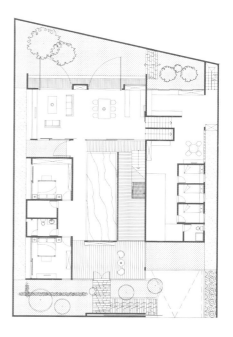

HOUSE 2, TANAH TEDUH
JAKARTA, INDONESIA
ANDRA MATIN ARCHITECT

'This house is about how to make design which is not too designed, but to make someone feel at home.'—Andra Matin

Tanah Teduh is a gated community comprising twenty houses. The master plan was drawn up by architect Andra Matin, who has also designed twelve of the houses. The others have been designed by eight individual architects, all from Indonesia, as part of a commitment to make the development fully local, for example, in using only local materials.

In the context of the debate about whether gated communities are really communities or not, Tanah Teduh is interesting in the way the planning respects the existing site and promotes community. None of the trees on the site were cut down. The topography, which descends at a relatively steep angle to a natural pond, was also preserved and no excavations allowed. The pond has been preserved and is cleaned by filtration and water plants. The planning involves an organic clustering of the houses, shared landscaping and generous communal facilities around the pond, such as a yoga room, community meeting place, barbeque facilities, pool, jogging track, children's playground and sun deck. Individual swimming pools are forbidden in order to bring people together around the communal pool.

House 2 is sited up on the hill near the entry to the complex. Its plot is irregular in shape, reflecting the organic, 'ungridded' character of the development. It is an L shape, designed in response to the wall of the compound next door, which is not a part of the complex. The programme is unusual in that the dining room/pantry is a free-standing pavilion surrounded by a moat, entered across a small bridge and giving the impression that the pavilion is floating on water. The house is set on a mound, borrowing the landscape of the house next door, including a magnificent kapok tree. It is set back precisely in order to allow this. The living room is located diagonally opposite across the garden so that people have to venture outside to get from one to the other.

The wall that leads directly from the dining pavilion and culminates at the entry door includes a powder room in addition to hiding services and the rather imposing next-door house. It is a custom-designed *keraunnarang* wall of faceted precast cement. Variations of this raw but highly decorative wall have been used throughout the complex and, along with the shared landscape, act as a unifying element. The result is that the complex is like a village where each house is different but where all of them somehow work together to form a community of buildings.

Left The completely glazed galleria overlooks the courtyard and links the guest bedrooms.

Top Looking back from the kapok tree, the house sits on a rise like a glowing jewel.

Right The long section shows how the house is situated within the sloping topography.

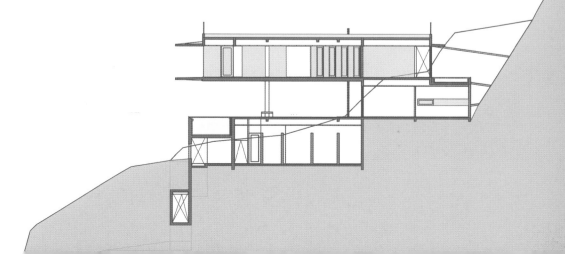

On the upper level of House 2, there is no air-conditioning in the circulation spaces, although individual rooms can be closed off and employ air-conditioning. These upstairs spaces are linked by an L-shaped glass gallery where the view is framed by a low soffit, at about head height, and a correspondingly low extended eave outside. This creates intimacy and a sense of privacy while still allowing a panoramic view to the outside.

The plan of the house has been generated by the existing trees, the neighbouring wall, whose textured and stained surface provides an intriguing contrast to the modernist white finishes of the house, and the aim of making living in the house much like living in the garden.

With guest rooms down one gallery, the master bathroom and bedroom are down the connecting gallery leading towards the view. The master bathroom opens on to an open-to-the-sky timber deck courtyard, a space shared by a free-standing bath tub and an existing tree thrusting up through the floor. This space is, in turn, connected to the walk-in wardrobe of the master bedroom which is part of the corridor, separated from it only by retractable curtains. The bedroom is fully glazed from floor to ceiling, with generous eaves. It opens on to a rooftop grassed terrace where another tree thrusts up through the roof. From here, there is an expansive view down to the pond.

Stand down by the kapok tree and look back up at the house and the dining pavilion and the house itself present as a gentle, intimate home, modest in scale. With its geometrical composition of white, intersecting planes and horizontal lines it is

Left From the roof terrace, there is an excellent view of the L-shaped galleria on the second level.

Below left Looking up from the next-door site, there is a clear view of the tree that thrusts up through the roof terrace.

Right Across the courtyard is a view of the decorative *keraunnarang* wall which is a unifying feature throughout the estate.

Below The downstairs sitting room is linked to a home office by pivoting timber doors.

Right The master bedroom is defined simply by a curtain and looks out to a timber deck and the rooftop garden terrace.

Below Entry to the house is up the side into the courtyard and is marked by a *keraunnarang* corner wall.

reminiscent of an earlier, European modernist tradition. The difference is that, inside, the glass and white concrete are complemented by the teak doors, window framing, joinery and detailing, locating the house firmly in its tropical context.

Minimal air-conditioning is enabled by cross-ventilation, water and a lush, encompassing garden. The L shape and the right-angled wall of the next-door property create a garden courtyard completely private from the neighbouring houses, but with enticing glimpses of the layered landscape beyond.

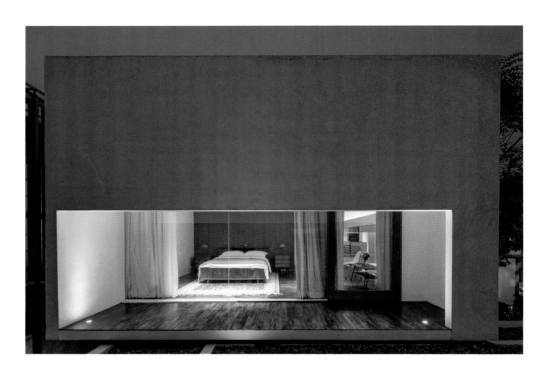

Above left The outdoor bath court accommodates an existing tree.

Above The master bedroom with its retractable curtain and view out to the rooftop green terrace.

Left Ground floor plan.

Below The galleria leading from the master bedroom back to the stairs.

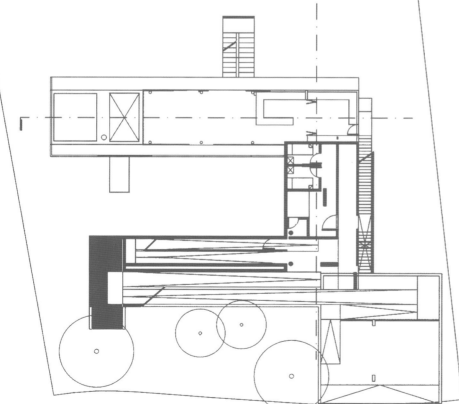

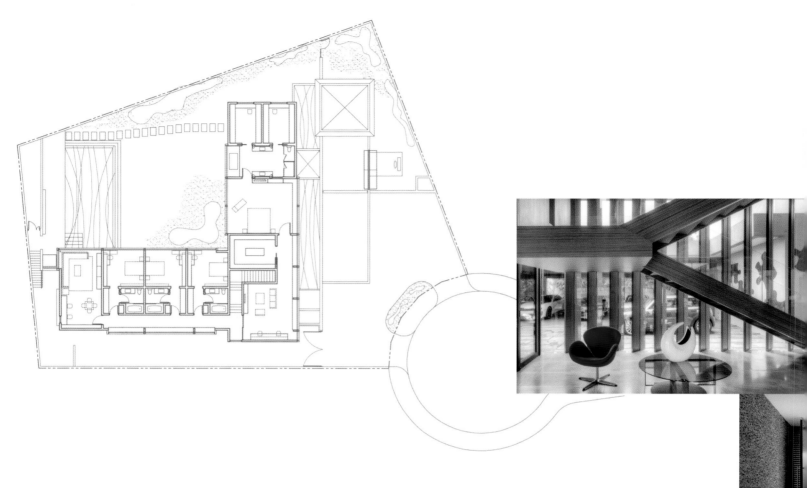

THE PHILIPPINES

PARAÑAQUE HOUSE
PARAÑAQUE, MANILA
ATELIER SACHA COTTURE

Right The house is masked from the street by an inventive use of treated bamboo screening.

Below right The section shows the artful distribution of volumes, including the setback of the top floor master bedroom.

Below The entry sequence involves moving through a stone vestibule and across a timber bridge into the courtyard.

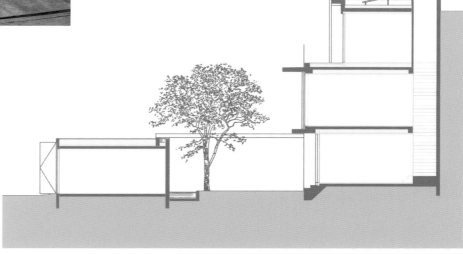

'I was not interested in seeing the outside because it is not a nice environment. I wanted my own little world.'—Sacha Cotture

Architect Sacha Cotture is French Swiss. Trained in Switzerland, he practised in Hong Kong for ten years before moving with his Filipino wife to Manila. The house he has designed for himself and his family is both a response to the climate and to the local culture.

On the one hand, the house references the traditional Filipino house, with a solid base and a light volume on top, along with an extensive use of local materials. On the other hand, it celebrates the imported Spanish courtyard typology.

Although the house is in a gated community, or exclusive village as it is often known in the Philippines, the built environment is messy and unattractive. Cotture's strategy was to block out the immediate environment as far as possible and create his own private green world.

From the street, therefore, the house gives little away. Screened by the garage, only the upper level with its façade of treated bamboo poles is visible. The scale was important, partly to respond to the low scale of the neighbourhood but also to respect the integrity of the courtyard plan. Hence, the long horizontal lines and the way the upper level is recessed make the ground floor, in effect, a podium for the upper level bedrooms.

Entry to the house is either from the garage or from a steel-framed timber door which leads into a cave-like transitional space with walls and floor of rough-hewn *araal*, a local granite, and lit by a pendant *capiz* mother-of-pearl lamp. This arrival sequence, a slow transition from the public to the private world, is extended by a timber-planked bridge across a moat that defines the courtyard garden. The bridge crosses a rhomboid-shaped pond with 'millionaire' vines hanging from a meshed, green canopy. From here, one either advances into a vestibule or turns right along the edge of the garden courtyard which is connected for its entire length to the glazed inside living space that steps up from the garden. At the end of this entry sequence is the *lanai*, the covered outdoor eating space, linked to the kitchen and breakfast bar.

For most of this journey, guests are protected from the sun by the concrete overhang from the living space, the deeply recessed *lanai* and the green canopy over the bridge.

The courtyard typology essentially makes use of previously unused perimeter space by bringing it inside and wrapping the house around it. Here, it means that a plot of 360 square metres can sustain a house of 400 square metres. By turning its back on the street and wrapping itself around a courtyard, the house becomes a refuge from the outside world. The courtyard then becomes a prospect out from the house, militating against any sense of claustrophobia. Pursuing this agenda, Cotture has created a green courtyard using local plants. A water wall washes into the moat and helps cool the house. On the roof of the garage, the architect has created a garden so that from the upper level bedrooms one can look down on to greenery rather than out to the scruffy neighbourhood. A green wall above the *lanai* screens the next-door house.

Above Looking down the courtyard to the *lanai*. Eventually, the next-door house will be fully screened by the green wall.

Below The floating stair treads become an abstract decorative feature.

Above The sheltered *lanai*, situated directly off the kitchen, is naturally cooled.

This remarkably imaginative and intimate house is notable for its extensive sustainable strategies. Cotture has used materials that are local, sustainable and inexpensive. The natural materiality of the treated bamboo on the façade complements the overarching modernist design intent, a strategy which works equally well inside where the bamboo poles are used as the stair barrier, filtering light into the living area and bringing the façade inside. Local mahogany is used throughout the house for joinery and for the bookshelves in the living area. Acacia is used for the carved timber furnishings, designed by Cotture to be both decorative and functional elements. Local *araal* granite is used for the walls and floor of the entry, with *romblom*, a local marble, used for flooring in the living area and the master bathroom. The synthetic render on the courtyard walls is a mix of adobe and crushed shell, a material

Right The kitchen steps down to the *lanai*.

that is widely used in the Philippines. The beautifully textured wall in the master bedroom wall is made up of cubes of coconut bark. The pendant lamps seen throughout the house are Filipino products, all made from *capiz* shell and help to generate a sense of aesthetic unity for the house. Solar panels and the combination of openness to the outside, water features and green space minimize the need for air-conditioning.

This house is highly sustainable from an environmental point of view, but equally culturally for the way it sustains continuity with traditional housing forms and uses local materials and craftsmanship, and socially for the way it shapes a clear identity for the family which lives there.

Given that it is a courtyard house, the scale was important, hence recessing the master bedroom and having the long horizontals.

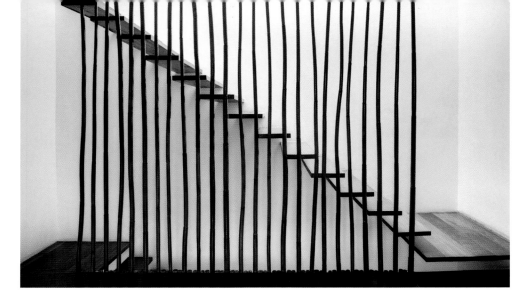

Left An imaginative use of treated bamboo poles to frame the floating timber staircase.

Right The master bedroom has a feature wall made up of coconut bark cubes.

Far right The master bedroom, which opens on to a terrace, can be closed off by a treated bamboo sliding door.

Below The living area with its customized *capiz* shell pendant lights.

Below Ground floor plan.

Right The rooftop terrace and corner window at the top of the stairs.

BATANGAS HOUSE
BATANGAS, THE PHILIPPINES
ARCHIPELAGO ARCHITECTS

Above The entry is a beautifully composed set of modernist white forms complemented by the timber garage door, talisay tree and through view to the ocean.

Left A view of the offshore islands from the roof terrace of the guest pavilion.

'I sat here on the property to define the essence of what I wanted it to be. Of course, the overarching element is the sea. I wanted to make that the focus and have the architecture take a step back, even down to the colour palette.'—Chut Cuervas

Ricardo (Chut) Cuervas completed graduate and post-architectural studies in the United States. He has been back in the Philippines and based in Manila for the last ten years where most of his work has been as a developer. This is the first landed house he has designed.

It is what is popularly known as a 'rest house' or holiday house. Located on the coast more than two hours' drive from Manila, it faces south and is in an area featuring a mix of holiday homes, small farms and fishing villages. Punta Fuego was formerly a sugar plantation and was first developed as a holiday village in the early 1990s with the stipulation that all the houses had to be designed in a 'Mediterranean' style. The Batangas House is one of the first allowed with a modernist aesthetic.

As the name Punta Fuego suggests—'fiery ridge'—its topography is a rocky ridge thrusting into a constantly changing seascape. The Cuervas family had previously owned a holiday home in the region but it had passed its use-by date. But they wanted to stay in this beautiful area which is noted for its series of points and coves, many with private sandy beaches.

The family had owned the Punta Fuego site for eight years before building. Shortly afterwards, they acquired the adjacent lot, on which they built a free-standing two-bedroom guest pavilion to create a unified complex with a total of eight bedrooms.

The strategy was deliberate. Although the house is intended to bring the family together, everyone wants their own room and wants to be able to invite their own friends to stay. Hence, the design brief was to create a family retreat while acknowledging the needs of individual family members. It is, says architect Chut Cuervas, 'the ultimate generational, multifunctional home'.

The Punta Fuego areas has an extreme climate. It is exposed to the salt air and is extremely hot in summer. Cuervas looked at boats as a guide to how to make a sustainable seaside home. This led him to avoid steel and use aluminum and timber instead. He also used indigenous local plants that are able to resist wind and salt, such as the seaside variety of the yuecca tree. For heat protection, especially given the extensive glazing, he used generous overhangs and fixed louvred sunscreens. The terraces off the two south-facing bedrooms form the overhangs for the downstairs, creating covered spaces for relaxing and entertaining.

From the street, the house is unassuming, partly because of the request to make it architecturally reserved, but also to serve a dramatic purpose. An existing talisay tree was retained and now provides a lush green canopy over the entry, counterpointing

Below Looking past the main house to the expansive lawn.

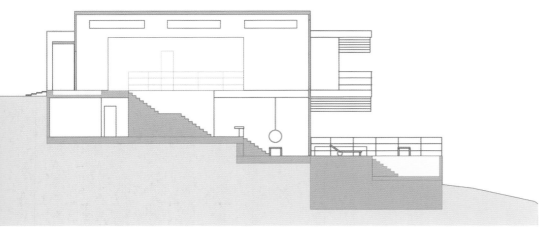

THE SUSTAINABLE ASIAN HOUSE

the minimalist and geometric front elevation where the entry exactly bisects the façade. A water feature at the entry has the same dimensions as the rear swimming pool to provide a thematic connection between front and back. The bridge which crosses this pond is the beginning of a very theatrical sequence of arrival. Once the doors are open, the sightline is directed straight through the central void to the triple-height glass wall and doors, with the central glass panel perfectly framing an island off the coast.

One then goes down a flight of travertine steps to a mezzanine where a long travertine breakfast bench, interrupted only by the stairs, continues to conceal the final stage of the arrival journey. With the kitchen and a television sitting room on either side, the stairs then continue down to the lower level where the living/dining area completes what is now a single fluid space before extending out to the deck, the pool and the majestic seascape—the climax of this highly dramatic procession from the entry.

The minimalist structure, the white palette and the extensive glazing ensure that the house 'dematerializes', creating the sense of living in a seascape rather than in a house. The planning also ensures an enormous amount of natural light and cross-ventilation.

This is a modern house for a modern family doing a very traditional thing—having a seaside holiday. Like all traditional holiday houses, it makes few demands either on the people living there or on energy resources.

Opposite above The house is essentially three pavilions, with the guest pavilion to the left and the bedrooms all set well back under protective overhangs.

Opposite below The section shows how the house steps down over a series of levels.

Below A sea view from the guest pavilion deck.

Above The kitchen and breakfast bar are level with a small television room at the end and a doorway leading outside to the guest pavilion.

Below Stepping down from the kitchen level to the dining area that leads directly to the outdoor sitting room.

Left Looking back up to the entry and grand stairway.

Below The dining and living areas have Kenneth Coponbue pendant lights which help to dematerialise the house.

Bottom The master bedroom is shaded by a generous overhang, allowing full appreciation of the magnificent views.

Left A small sitting room leads out to the lawn and guest pavilion.

Below The main living area is set below the kitchen level.

Left The travertine stairway with the island framed by a highlight window.

Below The outdoor sitting space is protected by a deep overhang with screening.

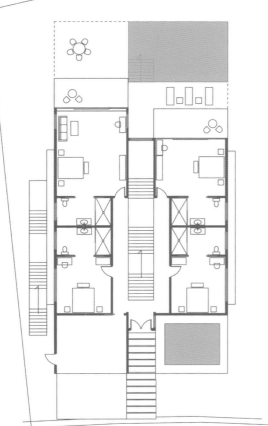

Above The powder room for the living and dining areas is extended to include a shower and small courtyard garden.

Left Entry level floor plan.

VIDAL HOUSE
LAGUNA DE BAY, THE PHILIPPINES
RENATO VIDAL

Right Sitting on an elevated corner site, the house pivots in two directions to maximize the views.

Below right Cross-section.

Below The house enjoys a magnificently elevated position with views across Laguna de Bay, with Manila in the distance.

'I didn't want a typical modern house. But it couldn't be too ornate or eclectic. It finally had to be something that could be appreciated by everyone.'—Renato Vidal

Renato Vidal is an internationally acclaimed Filipino artist, renowned for his home accessories, especially those using natural material such as grass and vines. His house on an exposed hill in the Ayala Greenfield Estates overlooking Laguna de Bay has been a collective creative project by Vidal and his friends Tony Gonzales, Milo Naval, Tess Pasola and Ponce Veridiano, and architect Denise de Castro. Depending on who you are talking to, it is a halfway house between Vidal's factory, six hours' drive away in the south, and his Manila apartment, or it is a place to house and display his art collection, or it is, in his own words, his 'retirement house'; this might mean retirement from the work force or, more likely, a place to retire in order to regain peace of mind, to collect his thoughts and to reconnect with himself in order to sustain his creative practice.

Certainly, the house has a meditative calm about it with its beautifully flowing and interconnecting spaces, its unerringly considered placement of art objects and its graceful relationship with its garden, designed by the iconic Filipino landscape artist Ponce Veridiano, and the panoramic views beyond.

Having been a compulsive collector of beautiful objects for many years, Vidal has nowhere to show them. Thus, the assemble of spaces—which is basically the story of the house—is designed to display these works of art, but also to serve the needs of a bachelor. It is not meant to be a family home, although the beautifully appointed guest amenities make it very welcoming to the visitor.

The house is an assembly of transparent cubic volumes generating multiple cross-views from room to room and from the inside to the outside with Veridiano's garden, the views to the lake and to Mount Makiling. These spaces work both vertically and in plan. Initially, the house presents as a modernist structure with its characteristic horizontal

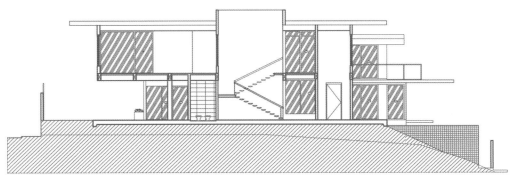

planes. But the striking palm-like glass sculpture by Vidal at the leading corner of the outside terrace (which seems to fit so snugly under the apparently cantilevered second floor but which happens to also disguise a supporting column) introduces a vertical element that is reinforced inside the house by the void above the dining room and the stairwell with its extraordinary mobile sculpture of suspended dark grey paper 'stones' by Tess Pasola.

The house has a white palette and is completely transparent, exemplified by the double-height living pavilion. But overhangs and the deeply recessed terrace, including the covered outdoor dining space at the rear of the house, reduce the heat load while still generating a lot of natural light. At the same time, the way the house can be opened up, the interior spine leading from the entry and the

covered space at the rear generate enough cross-ventilation to restrict air-conditioning to the bedrooms.

The white palette and largely glass skin also serve another purpose—to foreground the material qualities of the art works, because Vidal's taste runs to highly textured works of art which are then adroitly positioned to form a conversation with a collection of sleek, contemporary, iconic furnishings. In a sense, the house functions like a museum because its design enables each art work, object or piece of furniture to be appreciated for itself. Each object is celebrated for what it is, for its intrinsic quality and character rather than as a token of a brand. The sincerity and simplicity of Vidal himself is expressed through the house and the way it displays his collection. What is particularly intriguing

is the way this diverse collection seems to hold together as a unity, driven by the taste of the man who put it together.

Although there is a side entry to the rear of the house, the main entry is down the hill and up a ceremonial flight of steps. The entry porch features two massive granite Chinese timber shutters suspended above the entry terrace. The timber double doors at the entry are recycled traditional doors which still pivot off their original timber pins rather than a hinge and feature custom-designed handles by Filipino artist Impy Pilapil, who also has a suspended acrylic sculpture hanging in the dining room void. Once inside the vestibule, the house opens up, either to the left and into the living pavilion, straight ahead down the spine or to the right and a sitting room.

Left Floor-to-ceiling wrap-around glazing dematerializes the house so that inside and outside become one.

Right The pebble roof garden on the upper level.

Below As well as works of art, the house contains a collection of classic modern furniture and lighting.

A secondary staircase to the upper level leads off the spine, but the main stairway is adjacent to the living space. This culminates in a timber bridge overlooking the dining void and connecting to the guest bedroom. The bridge turns around and continues as a glass-balustraded gallery-cum-library past a high-backed antique Chinese chair to the master bedroom. Here, the Japanese aesthetic, which has so far been simply hinted at, becomes explicit in the way the bedroom steps up to a rooftop terrace, in the way a timber-louvred blind can be opened to reveal the Tess Pasola mobile in the stairway and in the mood of the bathroom with its timber 'Japanese' bath, actually a product of the Italian company Agape.

Apart from some specific items, such as the German e15 dining table, all the timber in the house is recycled, just as many of the art works reflect Vidal's preference for natural materials.

While the house has a number of environmentally sustainable features, it is most notable for its cultural sustainability, displaying the work of Filipino artists and supporting traditional craft while pulling together a diverse collection of old and new, raw and sophisticated art works, furnishings and lighting to make an argument for cultural continuity and universality. It is a house which highlights the value of materiality against the shallowness of materialism.

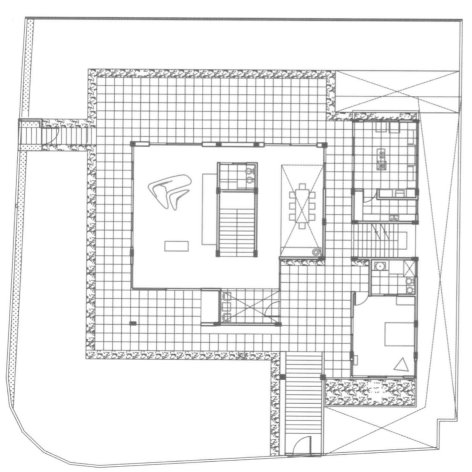

GOLF COURSE HOUSE
MANILA, THE PHILIPPINES
LOR CALMA DESIGN

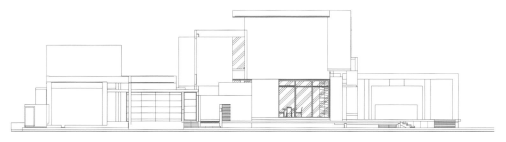

Left Cross-section.

Below The dynamic abstract patterning of the façade helps to generate air movement in and around the house.

Right The *lanai* and golf course seen from the upper verandah.

Below right Ground floor plan.

'When they brought me here and I saw it, I thought this is the best property I am ever going to be designing, fronting the golf course.'—Ed Calma

Of all the houses in this gated community, this is the only one to orient itself towards a beautifully verdant, undulating golf course with roaming deer and ducks. Despite the obvious benefits of a borrowed landscape view and access to prevailing winds, the local preoccupation with security predominates, with the other houses preferring to close themselves off to the outside although, ironically, the golf course (not associated with the gated community) is itself very well secured.

Ed Calma's clients wanted to open the house up. In fact, it was really their only requirement, apart from wanting a small house; this is 800 square metres in contrast to the Philippine average of 1,500 square metres. Calma split the property in two to

obtain a service area and the house. This enabled him to create a court entry with a garden on the golf course side. Apart from this, the planning was a response to contextual issues such as the passage of the sun, the prevailing winds and the view. By orienting the long eastern elevation of the house to the golf course, Calma was able to avoid direct exposure to the western sun and capture the prevailing winds that blow from the east in winter and from the northwest in summer.

The house, however, is approached from the street from where a typical Ed Calma strategy can be seen. The house presents as three cubic volumes—the car gallery (the client has a collection of classic cars and wanted to be able to display them to visitors), the service volume on the western

side of the house and the house proper—which step forward and up towards the golf course. The house volume, with its timber feature panels, is framed by the roof, which appears to float above the clerestory windows, and an extruded side panel with glimpses through to a tree in the garden court. This framing motif is repeated throughout the house to create a rhythmic unity. For example, floating and extruded frames apply to both the rear and the golf course façades of the house, even the balustrading of the bridge over the water feature at the entry to the house.

The downstairs living spaces are entered by way of a bridge over a *koi* pond and a transitional hall running down the side. Calma has exploited this by positioning the powder room so that it is the first

thing the visitor sees after turning left from the entry. With the door open, its glowing onyx basin stand becomes a beacon of welcome. Inside the house, the ground floor is completely open plan, essentially a long room with rhythmically placed piers clad in re-engineered veneer, open to the view and to breezes. On the western side, facing the court, angled vertical louvres and overhangs protect the interior of the house from the sun, while on the side facing the golf course the house shades itself to a large extent while allowing ample sun over the pool and lawn. This is helped by the upper terrace that runs the length of the house and acts as an overhang. At the northern end of the pool garden is a spacious *lanai* running directly off the dining area. This consists of a bar area, an outdoor dining space

Left The collection of classic cars can be seen looking through the timber screens of the living room.

Above The dark palette of the kitchen and bar adds an almost nightclub element to the expansive living/dining space.

Above The architect creates a rich façade composition across different planes using different colours and interlocking geometries.

Left The house is approached from the driveway by a bridge over a moat.

and a powder room and changing rooms whose granite screen acts as a decorative bookend to the garden court.

Upstairs, the rooms—three bedrooms, a family room, master bedroom and walk-in wardrobe—are assembled in a row linked on the outside by the terrace and inside by a corridor. These work in association with the clerestory windows, which acts as a wind chimney drawing warm air up and out, to ventilate the whole upper floor.

Teak timber from Thailand and Indonesia is used throughout the house with downstairs flooring of ceramic tile. Given the absence of sustainable forests in the Philippines, Calma used very little local timber.

The clients and their two children previously lived in a two-bedroom condominium apartment. According to Calma, 'they normally don't go outside', but once they moved in, they began to

Above The living area looking back to the kitchen/bar and dining area.

Left The architect's 'cubistic' strategy is most apparent from the street.

Opposite above The dining area leads directly out to the *lanai*.

Opposite below The *lanai* with the powder room and changing rooms behind.

appreciate the layout of the house and now utilize the outdoor spaces to the full. It is very much a validation of Winston Churchill's famous remark that 'we shape buildings, thereafter they shape us'. For example, the house's close connection to the golf course (from the house side the boundary wall is quite low, although from the gold course it is quite high because of the elevation of site) has led to a kind of extended community because the clients can greet and be greeted by many of their friends who use the golf course.

Orientation, shading strategies and openness mean that air-conditioning is necessary only at times when the wind falls away. At the same time, the house is socially sustaining because it has enabled the family to discover new ways of being together, sharing the unique site with friends and extended family, not to mention becoming *de facto* members of the golf club!

BOUGAINVILLEA HOUSE
DASMARIÑAS VILLAGE, MAKATI, THE PHILIPPINES
C/S DESIGN ARCHITECTURE

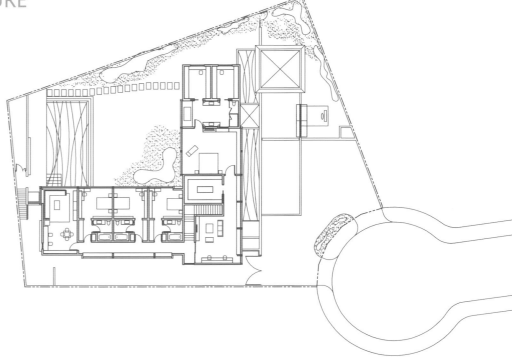

Right The ground floor plan shows the indirect arrival sequence, which sets up the final reveal of the verdant courtyard.

Opposite above The lush courtyard looking back to the *lanai*.

Opposite below The final point of arrival is across a bridge spanning a pond and through a stone portal.

'They are a family who like to feel they are outdoors and like to entertain outdoors. So, the way we laid out the house was that the outdoor living space became the centre of the home.'—Anna Maria Sy

The two themes running through this house are privacy and the outdoors, resulting in a courtyard typology. The irregular shape of the site assisted here because the small frontage gives no hint of the spacious grounds within. It also enabled architect Anna Maria Sy to position the guest bedroom as a separate pavilion directly off the entry vestibule with its own garden separate from the main garden, which also helps to maintain security for the main house.

Supporting the theme of privacy and security is the indirect arrival sequence which begins with a cobblestone driveway and *porte cochère*. This leads into a transitional space, a vestibule, which is entered through double-timber doors flanked by

vertical timber-louvred screens. The guest bedroom, a semi-public space, is directly ahead, so one turns left to approach the main house where the journey from the public to the private is extended by a bridge over a moat, a symbol of the final transition into the private realm.

The Bourgainvillea House is assembled around the grassed courtyard. It references the traditional Philippines house in that it has a solid masonry base and a timber upper level, here extruded to reinforce the sense of lightness by suggesting that it is floating, and also creating the impression that this is a galleria wrapping around the garden below. In fact, what we see are the bedrooms, all designed to look directly into the garden below, while the actual galleria is on the inside, linking all the upstairs spaces. This effect is mirrored at ground level where a recessed loggia connects the spaces along the long elevation leading down to the swimming pool.

In a crucial respect, however, the house differs from a traditional house where the internal procession would pass through a formal living room to the outdoor living *lanai* facing the garden. With the Bougainvillea House, however, the architect has turned that 'inside out and made the *lanai* the centre'. To walk over the bridge is to arrive in the *lanai* that connects the two wings of the house and faces the garden. The formal living room is to the right of the entry and its separation from the *lanai* is emphasized by having to step up into it, effectively making it a separate pavilion. The dining room is diagonally opposite the *lanai* off the loggia. The only entrance to the upper levels is a doorway off the *lanai* next to the powder room which can be locked at night and which makes a clear separation of public and private domains within the house.

To reinforce the sense of openness, the rear wall was pulled away from the house, allowing the pond

Left A cobblestone driveway leads to a *porte cochère* with steps leading up to the house entry.

Below The *lanai* looks straight down the garden courtyard to the pool.

to run down the back of the *lanai*, thus generating ample cross-ventilation through the main space. The wall continues past the bridge to complete the separation of the guest bedroom from the main house. This wall, made from stone from Kalatagan, which took months to make with local craftsmen hand cutting each small block, is mirrored at the other end of the garden where another stone wall backs the swimming pool. These walls bookend the garden court, with the rear wall brought forward to conceal services and make room for trees and bushes to screen out the neighbours. In this way, some land has been sacrificed in order to gain privacy. Lush plantings also run down the long side the garden, once again completely screening off the neighbours. 'From day one', says Anna Maria Sy, 'they did not want to see their neighbours.'

The project preferenced local materials where possible, using Almasiga timber and Indonesian tiles, although the external walls are travertine. The water feature is an effective cooling device, especially with cross-ventilation, and the spacious garden court ensures large amounts of natural light in all the rooms. From a social perspective, the house can be seen as sustaining the Filipino tradition of close families, but in a thoroughly modern way by providing clearly separated private spaces (bedrooms, the children's room on the ground floor), complemented by a well-positioned communal area to bring the family together.

Above left The arrival sequence from the *porte cochère* through double timber doors into a vestibule.

Above The upstairs living and entertainment room.

Below On entering the inner house, there is a small living room off to the right and opposite the *lanai*.

Above The *lanai* is backed by a large pond and a stone wall.

Top right The powder room off from the *lanai*.

Centre right The master bathroom is on the upper level.

Right The master bedroom.

Above Looking across the pool to the loggia.

Left The lush vegetation of the courtyard is designed partly as a cooling strategy, but also as a way to create privacy from the neighbours.

Right At night, lighting among the vegetation adds to the house lighting to create a magical effect.

THE ARCHITECTS AND DESIGNERS

AAMER ARCHITECTS

Aamer Taher was born in Singapore in 1962. He graduated in architecture from the National University of Singapore in 1987 before completing a Master of Architecture degree at the Architectural Association in London in 1990. He practised in London before returning to Singapore in 1992 to establish SAA Partnership, followed by the Aamer Taher Design Studio in 1994. He is a Corporate Member and Council Member of the Singapore Institute of Architects and a Member of the Royal Institute of British Architects. He is active on numerous committees and teaches in the Architecture School at the National University of Singapore.

Aamer Taher Architects is a small architectural firm that views design as finding an ideal solution to a combination of factors that include site, culture and climate, structure and services, with an economy of means to arrive at an aesthetic whole. The firm aims to reconcile function and beauty in design, backed by strong service and management support to ensure client satisfaction.

Archisculpture, architecture, landscape and interior installations—each project is seen as a work of art, conceived through a thorough appreciation of site, context and brief, and carefully sculpted to congenially fit into the site while keeping the client's brief intact.

AAMER ARCHITECTS
Aamer Taher, Peter Eimers
5 Burn Road, (Tee Yih Jia Food Building), #06-02, Singapore 369972
(65) 6280 3776, Peter Eimers' mobile 9615 5699
info@aamertaher.com
peter@aamertaher.com

ANDRA MATIN ARCHITECT

Born in Bandung in 1962, **Isandra (Andra) Matin** is one of Indonesia's most highly respected architects. He is a graduate of Parahyangan Catholic University, Bandung, and is currently Principal of Andra Matin Architects, established in 1998. Like many of his colleagues, Andra Matin is active across many fields of cultural activity. He is a member of Arsitek Muda Indonesia, a regular lecturer at universities and has participated in and curated numerous exhibitions. His work has been widely published internationally. Among his many awards are the 2008 Indonesian Institute of Architects Jakarta Award for the Conrad Wedding Chapel (in collaboration with Antony Liu)—one of five IAI awards—and the 2010 Green Design Award for Rumah Komunitas Salihara, Jakarta.

Most recently, he drew up the master plan for the Tanah Teduh estate in Jakarta. This highly innovative project involves 10 invited architects designing 20 houses in a sensitively landscaped community, with Andra Matin responsible for 9 of them.

ANDRA MATIN
Jalan Manyar 3, Blok 03 kav. 29-30 No. 4-6, Sektor 1, Bintaro Jaya, Jakarta 12330, Indonesia
(62 21) 735 3338
andra168@cbn.net.id

ARCHIPELAGO ARCHITECTS

Ricardo (Chut) Cuerva was raised in Manila in the Philippines but undertook his architectural training in the United States. He obtained a Bachelor of Architecture degree from the Southern California Institute of Architecture in 1998, then went on to complete a Master of Architecture degree at Colombia University. He then returned to the Philippines and from 2003 has worked for Nova Construction + Development. Nova, established in 1980, is a contracting firm specializing in single-family residences and small-scale commercial projects. However, it has also built 15 high-rise projects in the three central business districts of Metro Manila.

In 2005, Chut Cuerva established Archipelago Architects to allow him to pursue his interest in developing sustainable and modernist landed houses in a tropical climate.

ARCHIPELAGO ARCHITECTS
Ricardo C. Cuerva
Suite 3902, West of Ayala Building, 252 Gil Puyat Avenue, Makati City, The Philippines 1200
info@archipelago.ph

ATELIER SACHA COTTURE

Sacha Cotture is a Swiss architect now living in Manila in the Philippines where he is Principal of Atelier Sacha Cotture.

After obtaining his architectural diploma in Fribourg, Switzerland, and working for two years there, he moved to Hong Kong where he worked for several years in a large international practice involved in large-scale mixed-use developments and urban planning, principally on projects located in China, India and the Middle East.

After moving to Manila and establishing Atelier Sacha Cotture, he now operates his practice between Switzerland and the Philippines, with the practice focusing on medium-scale tailor-made residential and hospitality projects in both countries.

All projects are site-specific and concerned to reference the immediate cultural and architectural heritage, taking every opportunity to work with local, sustainable materials.

ATELIER SACHA COTTURE
c/o Aidea Philippines, 30/F Ayala Life FGU Centre, 6811 Ayala Avenue, Salcedo Village, Makati City 1227, The Philippines
sacha@ateliersachacotture.com

BEDMAR & SHI

Ernesto Bedmar was born in Argentina and completed his Bachelor of Architecture degree in 1980 at the University of Architecture and Town Planning at Cordoba in Argentina. He worked with Miguel Angel Roca in Argentina, moving in 1982 with the practice to Hong Kong to work on the Tai Long Wan Tourist Resort on Lantau Island. He relocated to Singapore in 1984, working initially with SAA Partnership before establishing his own practice, Bedmar & Shi Designers (with Patti Shi), in 1986, working across architecture, conservation, landscape and interior design.

The practice is active throughout Southeast Asia, although extending as far as New York, London, Hong Kong, Tibet, India and New Zealand, specializing in residential and hospitality design.

The practice has maintained a staff of 12 for many years and is a deliberately multicultural mix. The emphasis is on quality design and on exploring the relationship of buildings to nature. Bedmar & Shi's houses invariably have a close connection to the outside landscape, which is always carefully considered. Often it is a case not just of the house opening up to the outside but bringing the landscape into the house with water features and plantings. The practice's work always has a strong emphasis on materiality, using stone and timber. With the liberal use of water, subtle manipulation of light and a deft aesthetic sense, a Bedmar & Shi house always has a reassuring sense of calm while celebrating a unique form of contemporary tropical residential architecture.

The practice has received many awards and is much published. It has published two monographs of its own on the practice, *Romancing the Tropics* (2007) and *Five in Five* (2011).

BEDMAR & SHI
Ernesto Bedmar
12A Keong Saik Road, Singapore 089 119
(65) 6227 7117
bedmar.shi@pacific.net.sg

BUDI PRADONO ARCHITECTS

Budi Pradono has practised as an architect since 1995. His search for an architectural identity has involved extensive travel and collaboration with artists and architects from many countries. He began his career at an architectural consulting company in Sydney, 1995–6. In 2002, he won the Bunka Cho Fellowship Award. From 2000 to 2002, he worked in Japan with Kengo Kuma & Associates. He then returned to study, attending the Berlage Institute, Laboratory of Architecture in Rotterdam in 2002–3. This brought him into contact with architects such as MVRDV, Monolab, Herzog & de Meuron, FOA (Foreign Office Architects) and Zaha Hadid. He also attended a studio run by Winy Maas, principal architect at MVRDV, resulting in an exhibition of the studio's work at the 1st Biennale of Architecture in the Netherlands.

As a result of his exposure to these architects, Budi concluded that he did not believe in the 'one man show architect' as it was during the era of Le Corbusier or Tadao Ando. As a result, the office of Budi Pradono Architects uses three strategies on its projects: programming study with CAD media, sketch-up (3D), spatial study with model or scale model, and material study by building a mock-up at 1:1 ratio. Budi Pradono is active in competitions and lectures extensively at private and public universities in Indonesia. His projects have been published in books and magazines and exhibited at arts and architectural events both domestically and overseas. Award-winning projects include the Tetaring Kayumanis restaurant at Nusadua in Bali, and the restaurant at Jimbaran in Bali which was winner of the Commercial Built Project Award and Commended in the Leisure Future category in the Cityscape Architectural Review Award, Dubai, in 2004. It was also given an Honorable Mention at the AR Awards for emerging architecture, London, in 2005. In 2006, Budi Pradono received the Silver Medal of UIA at the Bulgarian Triennale of Architecture in 2006

BUDI PRADONO ARCHITECTS
Budi Pradono
Jl Walet 6, Blok I.2 No.11, Sektor 2 – Bintaro Jaya, Jakarta 12330, Indonesia
(62 21) 737 0367
Mobile (62) 813 1122 3997
info@budipradono.com

CHAT ARCHITECTS

Chatpong Chuenrudeemol is director of Chat Architects, established in 2012. Chat received his Bachelor of Arts in Architecture from the University of California Berkeley in 1994 and completed his Master of Architecture at Harvard University's Graduate School of Design in 2000. In between his two degrees, he worked at Fernau and Hartman Architects in Berkeley for two years. His work experience also includes a position at Boston's Office dA after graduating from Harvard. In early 2001, Chat moved back to Bangkok in order to pursue an independent practice and to teach architectural studio at King Mongkut University of Technology at Thonburi.

In 2004, Chat formed b/A/R, or bangkok Architectural Research, with partner Varoot Samalapa, an office which combined design and research, solving design problems from interiors to architecture and urban planning/design. Chat Architects continues that interdisciplinary mix.

Projects include a variety of residential and commercial designs. The office rigorously sees projects through from conceptual development all the way to the completion of construction. The complete supervision of all stages of design allows the office to develop a hands-on approach to design. The practice has enjoyed wide recognition and has received a number of awards. It has been widely published, locally and internationally. The Ekamai Residence was selected as one of the '2009 Houses of the Year' by *Baan La Suan* magazine.

The practice also carries out research projects in the field of urban planning, construction and design. In doing so, it not only provides information as a product to its clients but is able to continually update its own database of knowledge in information of design and construction.

CHAT ARCHITECTS
Chatporn Chuenrudeemol
266/1 Soi Ekamai 18, Sukhumvit 63 Road, Bangkok 10110, Thailand
(667 2) 6681 657 0455
chat_chuenrudeemol@hotmail.com
www.chatarchitects.com

CS ARCHITECTURE

CS Architecture is an architecture, interior design and consulting firm established in 1992, based in Redding, Connecticut. Its partners, Jason Chai and Anna Maria Sy, established CS Design Consultancy in Manila in 1994 in response to increasing demand for services throughout Asia. Currently, the firm handles a wide range of corporate, commercial, educational and residential projects in North America and Southeast Asia.

The common thread in the work of CS Architecture is a recognition of local architectural heritage, building traditions, climatic conditions and, especially, the particular needs of the clients. The practice has been widely published in magazines and books in the United States, Philippines, Australia, Singapore and Korea.

Anna Maria Sy was educated at Harvard University in the Graduate School of Design. She holds a Master of Architecture (1989) from Columbia University, Barnard College, and a Bachelor of Arts (1984). She is the Managing Director of CS Design Consultancy. Prior to establishing the practice, she was a design architect in the Los Angeles office of Skidmore, Owings and Merrill, responsible for design and construction documentation on projects ranging from beachfront hotels to corporate interiors and amusement parks. She now heads the operations of the

THE ARCHITECTS AND DESIGNERS *continued*

Manila office with responsibilities including single-family and high-rise condominium residences, commercial buildings, corporate interiors and institutional facilities.

Jason J. Chai studied at Harvard University School Graduate School of Design. He holds a Master of Architecture (1988) from Columbia College, Columbia University, and a Bachelor of Arts (1983). He is Managing Director of CS Architecture LLC, USA, and previously worked for several high-profile design firms in Boston, New York and Los Angeles. As design architect with Skidmore, Owings and Merrill, he participated in the design of high-rise condominiums, hotels, office buildings and corporate interiors. Since beginning his collaboration with Anna Maria Sy, he has expanded the firm's area of expertise to include educational facilities and customized residences. He brings to the practice a high level of experience in construction as the founding partner of a turnkey design-build firm from 1992 to 1999.

C/S ARCHITECTURE
Jason Chai, Anna Maria Sy
Lapanday Center, Unit 303, 2263 Don Chino
Roces Avenue Ext., Makati City, The Philippines
(63 2) 893 0555
mail@csarchitecture.com

CSYA PTE LTD

Chan Sau Yan (Sonny) was born in 1941 in Kuala Lumpur, Malaysia. He had his primary, secondary and tertiary education in Malaysia and the United Kingdom, graduating as an architect in 1963 from the Northern Polytechnic of London. He later completed post-graduate Tropical Studies at the Architectural Association in 1964, after which he worked in London with Arup Associates. He moved to Singapore in 1965, establishing Kumpulan Akitek before establishing his present practice as Chan Sau Yan Associates in 1993. In 2011, Chan Sau Yan Associates was incorporated and is now known as CSYA Pte Ltd.

Sonny Chan's experience encompasses a wide range of residential, commercial, institutional, recreational and tourism-related projects across the region and elsewhere.

He was a founder member of the Singapore Planning and Urban Research Group and has been an external tutor, examiner and adjunct associate professor in the School of Architecture at the National University of Singapore, external critique with Universiti Malaya as well as serving in professional institutes and other government institutions in various capacities. He has received several architectural awards for design distinction, including the prestigious President's Design Award 2011.

CSYA provides full architectural services, including master planning, concept and detailed design, documentation and supervision, in addition to a full interior design service. The firm, which is active regionally and internationally, is committed to design innovation and the integration of appropriate technology. It firmly believes that design excellence requires the close and active collaboration of the client supported equally by the skills of the specialist consultants.

CSYA PTE LTD
Sonny Chan
5 Keong Saik Road, Singapore 089113
(65) 6324 3128
nor@csya.com

D-ASSOCIATES

Established in 2001, d-Associates is a Jakarta-based architectural practice directed by Gregorius Supie Yolodi and Maria Rosantina. The practice has become prominent in Indonesia with a range of carefully detailed material experimentations and meticulously executed architectural projects. The firm's work has been widely awarded and published internationally.

After obtaining a degree in architecture in 1998 from the Faculty of Architectural Engineering of the University of Parahyangan, one of the oldest and most respected schools of architecture in Indonesia, and spending a period of internship at Grahacipta Hadiprana in Jakarta and Triacoin Sanur, Bali, **Gregorius Supie Yolodi** was a partner at Tjipta Nuansa Kreasitama architectural consultants between 1999 and 2000. In 2001, he established d-Associates in Jakarta. Supie served as the Head of Professional Practice of the IAI Jakarta Branch between 2006 and 2009. He also actively participates in the Young Indonesian Architects' forums and design workshops. He has established a reputation as one of the leading architects of his generation based on his pursuit of new trajectories in formal architectural composition within contemporary design discourses in tropical Indonesia and Southeast Asia.

Maria Rosantina graduated from the same architectural school as Supie in 1998. She completed an internship at Rekamatra in Bandung, subsequently working in Hepta in Bandung and Batara Mega Krida Kencana in Jakarta. In 2003, Maria joined d-Associates as design partner. She brings to the practice a strong sensitivity for architectural tectonics and proportions, and a passion for a play of textures and material experimentation.

Both Supie and Maria were active members of the Green Architecture club during their studies and are well-travelled throughout the Indonesian archipelago, an experience that has given them a strong awareness of the architectural history, traditions, and socio-urban and environmental characteristics of their rapidly developing nation.

D-ASSOCIATES
Gregorius Supie Yolodi, Maria Rosantino
Jalan Bangka XI A, Pela Mampang, Jakarta Selatan, Indonesia
(62 21) 7183214
info@d-associates.com

DESIGN COLLECTIVE ARCHITECTS

Design Collective Architects and their associated interior design practice, Essential Design Integrated, are based in Petaling Jaya on the outskirts of Kuala Lumpur. The firm is headed by **David Chan Weng Cheong** (Director), **Cha Mei Chun** (Director) and **Chan Mun Inn** (Director). A relatively young practice, they specialize in high-end residential design and commercial practice. Their residential work includes individual bungalows and small-scale boutique residential developments.

DCA describe their practice as 'process-based architecture' because it is based on a highly developed process of analysis and relationship-building with their clients. This begins with an analysis of the site and a thorough understanding of the clients, their values, their way of life and what they are looking for in a building. The analysis involves addressing aesthetic, practical and environmental issues. The synthesis of these key components results in a successful design. David Chan comments that, as architects, they are not designing houses for themselves but for their clients. Every house is unique and crafted to match the beliefs and dynamics of each client. Collaboration is essential in this process and includes not only close collaboration with the client but also between architects, interior designers and landscape designers. Hence, DCA is an integrated practice which aims to achieve aesthetic, functional and spatial unity in their houses.

DCA
David Chan
17B, Jalan 55 22/19 Damansara Jaya, Petaling Jaya, Selangor, Malaysia
(60) 7727 0199
david@dca.com.my

HAN AWAL ARCHITECTS

Yori Antar is the Principal of Han Awal Architects. The firm was established in 1970 by his eminent architect father, Han Awal, with Yori Antar joining the practice in the 1980s. Yori initially studied mechanical engineering before switching to architecture at the University of Indonesia. He was a founding member of the Young Architect Indonesia Forum and is a member of the Association of Indonesian Architects. Han Awal, an integrated practice ranging from architecture to urban planning with a staff of 36, is strongly committed to socially responsible practice.

Yori Antar is typical of his generation of Indonesian architects because of the wide scope of his activities—architect, educator, photographer and writer. Deeply committed to conserving indigenous culture, his current project,

Rumah Asuh, begun in 2008, is helping to sustain traditional building techniques and the associated traditional culture in some of the outlying islands of Indonesia, such as Flores, Nias and Sumba. In 2012, he won an Excellence Award at the UNESCO Asia-Pacific Heritage Awards for Cultural Heritage Conservation for a traditional house at Waerebo Village on Flores.

HAN AWAL ARCHITECTS
Yori Antar
Jalan Palem Puri #7, RT03/RT06 Serua Poncol – Sawah Baru, Ciputat-Tangerang (Bintaro Jaya Sektor IX), Indonesia
(62 21) 74577797, 7456 697, 7454 397
chirasumendap@gmail.com

K2LD

Ko Shiou Hee is the principal of K2LD Architects which he founded with David Lee in 2000. The firm has its main office in Singapore and another office in Melbourne.

Ko Shiou Hee is a graduate of Rice University in the United States. Following graduation, he worked for Morphosis in Los Angeles, Kohn, Pedersen, Fox & Associates and I. M. Pei & Partners in New York, and was architectural design consultant for the Zenitaka Corporation in Tokyo where he designed several prestigious buildings and won numerous international competitions. Returning to Singapore, he worked for Architects 61, has taught at the National University of Singapore and lectured extensively.

K2LD now works across multistorey high-rise commercial and residential developments, civic buildings, railway works and private residences. Its design philosophy is summed up by the expression 'Sense and Sensibility in

Architecture'. Sense refers to the intricate relationships between time, light and materials leading to spatial freedom. Sensibility concerns understanding how the natural beauty of materials can be brought out in construction. K2LD believes that design emerges from an intensive dialogue with clients and a sensitive study of the site and the client's brief. 'We are driven', they say, 'by design intent and not shackled to a predetermined style. Beauty and freedom are born out of the intensive process of creation and continuous refinement of ideas and structure intimately connected to space, function and context.'

K2LD ARCHITECTS
Ko Shiou Hee
261 Waterloo Street, Singapore, 180261
(65) 6738 7277,
info@k2ld.com

KANOON STUDIO

Born in 1971, **Chartchalerm Klieopati-non** studied architecture at Silpakorn University in Bangkok and continued his education at the Architectural Association in London. He established Kanoon Studio in 1999, and has produced designs for projects of varying scales, ranging from small merchandising projects to larger-scale residential communities. Trying to keep the practice dynamic, Chartchalerm engages himself in teaching design studios at his alma mater and enters various design competitions. In 2006, Kanoon Studio won First Prize for the Red Cross Children's Village in Nakorn Pathom.

Known for simple but meticulous designs, Kanoon Studio has become a representative for the new generation of Thai architects who address the gap

between global and local practices, responding to the particulars of each changing environment and attempting to propose a design that is appropriate through its order and tactile through its meaning.

KANOON STUDIO
Chartchalerm Klieopatinon, Vasuvat Mettapun
37 Soi 41 Rama IX Road, Suanluang, Bangkok 10250, Thailand
(66 2) 678 8322
kanoonstudio.multiply.com
kanoonstudio@yahoo.com

LOR CALMA

Lor Calma Design is an integrated design practice including architecture, space planning, interiors, furniture and lighting. The practice was founded by **Lor Calma**, who is an architect, sculptor, jewellery designer and furniture designer. Lor's son, Eduardo (Ed) became associated with the firm as early as 1991, becoming Design Director in 2008.

Ed Calma studied at the Pratt International Studies University in Rome in 1985 before taking a Bachelor of Architecture degree at the Pratt Institute in New York in 1988. He then completed a Master of Science in Advanced Architectural Design at Columbia University, New York, in 1994. He worked in New York for Ellerbe Becket, 1988–94, and Giovannini & Associates, 1990–1.

Ed Calma has received many awards, including the 2005 Gold Medal for Design at Expo 2004 in Aichi, Japan, the Gold Medal for Design at Expo 2008 in Zaragoza, Spain, and the 2008–9 International Category Award and First Place Award for Contemporary Kitchen Design in the Overall Sub-Zero and Wolfe Kitchen Design Contest at Expo 2008 in Zaragoza, Spain.

Ed Calma's approach to design is consistently innovative and modernist. The aim is to create timeless design, while in architecture his houses are characterized by a single, clear idea, lending the house an immediately recognizable identity.

LOR CALMA DESIGN INC
Eduardo Calma
G/F State Condo 1, 186 Salcedo Street, Legaspi Village, Makati City 1229, The Philippines
(63 2) 817 8465
info@lorcalma.com

MARRA & YEH ARCHITECTS

Marra + Yeh Architects was formed as a studio practice in 2000, working in community development, urban design and residential projects in the USA. In 2005, the practice relocated to Sydney and also established an office in Malaysia, working on urban, rural and remote area projects.

The practice is a partnership between **Ken Yeh** and **Carol Marra** who met while studying at the University of Texas at Austin. After working in Seattle, they moved to Australia. The practice is skilled in delivering a variety of project types, ranging from individual residences to commercial offices, master plans, retreats and resorts. They believe that architecture is the response to the uniqueness of each client and each place. They take a considered approach—of potential and constraints, the general and the particular, technology and tradition, aspirations and appropriateness. The practice specializes in understanding place, climate and client to create sustainable, crafted, delightful environments. It takes a very hands-on approach during construction, working closely with

builders and craftsmen to improve the final outcome. The practice was awarded a Churchill Fellowship in 2009 and has received a number of awards, including the 2001 Interior Lighting Design Award for the Issaquah Library, the 2005 AIA Design Award for the 911 Emergency Centre, and the 2005 AIA Design Award for the Issaquah Library

MARRA + YEH ARCHITECTS
Carol Marra, Ken Yeh
136B Shepherd Street, Darlington, NSW, Australia
(61 2) 9319 3899 (Sydney), (60 16) 308 6682 (Studio Asia), (60) 17 560 5655 (Ipoh office)
info@marrayeh.com

RENATO VIDAL et al

From modest beginnings as a basket weaver, **Renato Vidal** has established himself as one of the Philippines' leading craftsmen, creating a company with a global reach. His 25-year-old export company, First Binhi, is named after the *binhi* (seed in Filipino).

Renato grew up in the remote provincial town of Labo, Camarines Sur, the son of a rice and coconut farmer and a housewife. He moved to Manila to take up a pre-medicial course on the way to his dream of being a doctor, but while there also immersed himself in the arts. He became a fan of one of the Philippines' greatest sculptors, Anastacio Caedo, as well as enamoured of the works of the American artist Jamie Wyeth. He immersed himself in art, attending art shows and visiting museums, becoming a passionate art scholar, reading up on art subjects and hanging out in the Caedo studio as the maestro's informal apprentice, even studying Chinese brush painting.

His father's illness forced Renato to

return home to Labo and find work to help his family. His mother gave him the idea of producing rattan baskets to sell to handicraft exporters in Manila. Even then an astute innovator, Renato decided to make not just rattan baskets but use all the other natural materials growing around his home to fashion wonderfully handcrafted baskets of fern, grass, vines, twigs, fibre and bark. Renato is now known for his sculptural objects for the home fashioned from natural materials.

Renato often works collaboratively, as in the design of his own home, which is the collective result of working with architect Denise de Castro, architect and furniture designer Milo Naval, designers Tony Gonzales and Tes Pasola and landscape artist Ponce Veridiano. The house is also a home for his stunning art collection, his collection of modern furniture and lighting classics and his library, including almost everything ever published on Andrew and Jamie Wyeth.

RENATO VIDAL
(63) 916 224 6849/ (63) 916 561 7180
firstbinhi@yahoo.com.ph

Denise de Castro is a graduate of the MIT Architectural and Furniture Design Studios, Wellesley College, and Harvard Graduate School of Design where she qualified with a Master in Architecture degree in 2003. She established her own architecture and interior design company, DD Design, in Manila in 2003. She has also worked for Lor Calma Design Associates in the Philippines as a project architect from 2003 to 2005. In addition to her architectural and interior design work, she has also been involved in a variety of exhibition work, including the Philippine pavilion at Expo 2005 and the Tadashi Kawamata Boston Project, 2001.

DENISE DE CASTRO DESIGN
Unit 901B, Park Trade Center, 1716 Investment Drive, Madrigal Business Park, Muntinlupa, 1780, The Philippines
(63 2) 842 3059,
ddecastro_design@yahoo.com

Tony Gonzales, who developed the architectural design concept for the Vidal House, was born in 1961 in Davao, Philippines. He initially studied advertising before working with established Filipino artists in painting and printmaking. He was lured to paper early on, examining it from every perspective. In 1991, he helped establish GSG Industries, a handmade paper company, where he directed product design and development. From 1995 to 2007, Gonzales assisted the Philippine Department of Trade and Industry's Center for International Trade, Expositions and Missions in their merchandise development consultancy programmes, developing various products, curating exhibitions and winning Japan's Good Design Award for three of his designs. In 2000, he was one of the founders of Movement 8, a collective of Philippine designers who manufacture their own furniture and home accessories.

TONY GONZALES
c/o mindmasters@tri-lsys.com

Milo Naval studied architecture at the University of Santo Tomas and later interior design at the Philippine School of Interior Design. He worked initially in residential interior design, later becoming involved in commercial, corporate, hospitality and retail interior design. After 15 years, he established Evolve Designs and OMO Furniture and Accessories, designing and manufacturing contemporary and modern furniture and accessories. His furnishings use natural, indigenous materials and have been described as being 'clean, clear and free of fuss'. His products have been exhibited at numerous international fairs, including Valencia, Maison et Objet in Paris, ICFF in New York, I Salone in Milan and IMM in Cologne, and he exports all over the world. Milo Naval was a founding member of Movement 8, the alliance of Filipino designers which promoted Filipino design to the world. He is currently a member of the Board of Trustees and the Vice-President for Design of the Chamber of Furniture Industries of the Philippines.

MILO NAVAL
milonaval@gmail.com

Tes Pasola is a Manila-born paper artist, product designer and space stylist. She received a degree in Bachelor of Science in Fine Arts, majoring in Advertising, at the University of Santo Tomas in the Philippines. She is president of her 40-year-old company, Mind Masters, Inc., that exports paper-based products. She is also owner and president of TESP Draft Hub, a company that handles her space styling and graphic design projects.

Tes Pasola is creative consultant to many companies, and her designs use both paper and non-paper as materials She was co-founder of Movement 8, a loose alliance of Filipino designers whose mission was to promote Filipino design to the world. She is often commissioned for curatorships for FAME exhibits organized by the Center for International Trade Expositions and Missions. In April 2005, she was engaged to head a pioneering 'cross- breeding project' for Swarovski which led to an exhibition

entitled 'Crystal Fantasies' at one of Manila's most prestigious museums, the Ayala Museum. Her work was subsequently exhibited at the 'Swarovski Crystals for Paper' launch in Paris and Tokyo.

TES PASOLA
mindmasters@tri-lsys.com

Ponce Veridiano is a well-known landscape artist in the Philippines, although he was trained as an electrical engineer. It was a passion for plants which launched him on a career as a landscape artist. His first project was the Pearl Farm Beach Resort in Samal Island owned by the prominent family of Tony Boy Floirendo from Davao. While working in the family of Floirendo, Ponce was treated like a member of the family. As a result, he met other prominent families like the Zobel, Ayala, Soriano, Cojuangco, Araneta, Chua and more, all of whom asked him to design their gardens.

His creative mind and strong passion for native plants resulted in a true paradise in his own hometown in Nagcarlan, Laguna. This is a tropical house with a two-bedroom guest villa surrounded by different kinds of bamboo and tropical plants. Working with world class architects such as the Locsins, Mañosa, Conrad Onglao, Ed Ledesma and Ramon Antonio, he developed his skills in architecture and Interior design. Ponce is in high demand and works on both residential and commercial projects. Among his significant recent commercial projects is the Greenbelt mall in Makati City, Manila.

PONCE VERIDIANO
(63) 917 881 05788
ponceveridiano@yahoo.com.ph

RICHARD HO ARCHITECTS

Richard Ho graduated from the National University of Singapore in 1981 and worked with William Lim Associates and Kerry Hill Architects before venturing to Austria and Italy in 1985 where he spent six years working as an architect, the last two years with Aldo Rossi before returning to Singapore in 1991 to set up Richard Ho Architects.

Over the past 20 years, Richard Ho has received numerous awards for his work on conservation projects. He was the first Singaporean architect to receive the ARCASIA (Architects Regional Council of Asia) Gold Medal, three SIA (Singapore Institute of Architects) Design Awards and four URA Architectural Heritage Awards.

Richard's practice believes in using architecture as an expression of the continuity of the history of civilization and the memory of our cities. His practice strives to achieve an architecture that resonates with man's unending endeavour to be in harmony with his soul and the world he lives in.

The work of Richard Ho is characterized by deeply considered spatial organization and highly refined finishes. In the area of conservation work, the practice has been outstanding in the way it has been able to sustain the original character of buildings while reinventing them as contemporary homes, each one carefully calibrated to the clients and their values.

RICHARD HO ARCHITECTS
Richard Ho
691 East Coast Road, Singapore 459 057
(65) 6446 4811
info@richardhoarchitects.com

RT+Q ARCHITECTS PTE LTD

RT+Q is a deliberately small practice founded in 2003 by **Tse Kwang Quek**, a graduate of the National University of Singapore, and **Rene Tan**, a graduate of Yale and Princeton Universities in the United States who subsequently worked for Ralph Lerner and Michael Graves before returning to Singapore to work with SCDA Architects, 1996–2003.

The practice is committed to an architecture based on clarity of form, transparency of spaces and articulation of structure, along with a respect for the client's aspirations. The practice aims to speak in its own design language, one that is grounded in a search for shapes and forms akin to plastic sculptural art. The practice has worked in Malaysia, Singapore and Indonesia, from small homes to condominiums, resorts, offices and commercial buildings.

The work of the practice has been widely published and has received numerous SIA and PAM awards, including the Singapore President's Award in 2009. Both partners teach extensively at the National University of Singapore and La Salle College of the Arts in Singapore, the University of Hong Kong and Berkeley and Syracuse Universities in the US.

RT+Q ARCHITECTS
Rene Tan, Tse Kwang Quek
32A Mosque Street, Singapore 059510
(65) 6221 1366, mobile 9694 0851
admin@rtnq.com rtnq.com

SCOTT WHITTAKER

Scott Whittaker is Group Executive Director and Founding Partner of Design Worldwide Partnership (dwp). Born and educated in Australia, he holds a Bachelor of Architecture degree. Moving to Asia in

1994, with his business partners he has transformed dwp from a local Thai-based company to a pan-Asian company employing over 450 multicultural professionals in 12 offices in 10 different countries.

Dwp is a one-stop integrated design service delivering architecture, interior design, planning consultancy and project management across borders and across industries and disciplines. The company is divided into three portfolios—lifestyle, community and work—with a worldwide network of studios aiming to provide diversity, flexibility and creativity while delivering innovative, high-quality design solutions. Scott oversees all group creative activity at dwp.

SCOTT WHITTAKER (DWP)
Dusit Thani Building Level 11, 946 Rama IV Road, Silom, Bangkrak, Bangkok 10500, Thailand
(66 2) 267 3939, mobile (66) 8182 32965
scott.w@dwp.com

TRISTAN AND JULIANA STUDIO

Tristan and Juliana Studio was formally established in 2012. However, Juliana and Tristan have collaborated extensively since 2008. Born in Singapore, **Tristan Tan** established Cream showroom (1998–2009), a pioneer in Singapore for high-quality design-driven homewares. From 2010 to 2011, he collaborated with the Sunlight Group to start up the furniture showroom P5. From 2006 to 2012, he ran his own interior design studio, Tristan T.

Juliana Chan was born in Singapore and is an architecture graduate from the National University of Singapore. After an internship at HYLA Architects in Singapore, she undertook further training at the Royal Melbourne Institute of

Technology in Australian between 2002 and 2003. From 2004 to 2012, she worked at Bedmar & Shi in Singapore.

Tristan and Juliana Studio has undertaken numerous commercial and residential interior design commissions as well as residential renovations and new builds.

TRISTAN & JULIANA STUDIO
Tristan Tan, Juliana Chan
2 Brookvale Walk, 05-07, Singapore 599952
(65) 6680 0850
Juliana-chan@live.com, tristan-tan@live.com

VASLAB ARCHITECTURE

Vasu Virajsilp established VaSLab Architecture with Boonlert Deeyuen in 2003 and continues as Managing Director. He was born in Nashville, Tennessee, in the United States in 1972 and undertook his architectural studies in the US, earning a Bachelor of Architecture (with Honours) from the Pratt Institute in Brooklyn, New York, and his Master of Science in Advanced Architectural Design from Columbia University, New York.

Returning to Thailand after completing his studies, he worked initially with Tandem Architects in Bangkok in 1997. He later sought further experience in the US, working with Gerner Kronick & Valcarcel Architects in New York, 2001–2. He has also been a Visiting Instructor in the Faculty of Architecture and Planning, Master Architectural Design Studio at Thammasat University, Assumption University and Rangsit University between 1998 and 2009.

VaSLab is a design-oriented practice covering architecture, interior design and urban design. Much of their inspiration comes from modern art, notably Cubism,

abstraction, Dada, Surrealism and Deconstructivism. Whatever the scale, the practice always looks to invest innovation and experiment to make each project unique within its own context. They are particularly interested in the forces found in the site and in how competing forms can interact to generate unique spaces and building forms. This is one reason why the practice has taken a special interest in concrete and its potential for form-making,

VASLAB ARCHITECTURE
Vasu Virajsilp
344 Soi Sukhumvit 101, Sukhumvit Road, Bangjak, Prakanong, Bangkok, 10260, Thailand
(66 2) 741 8099, mobile 66 (0) 81 8759 457
vaslab@vaslabarchitecture.com

W ARCHITECTS PTE LTD

Mok Wei Wei graduated with a Bachelor of Architecture (Hons.) degree from the National University of Singapore in 1982. After working in partnership with William Lim at William Lim and Associates, and following the retirement of William Lim, Mok Wei Wei recast the company as W Architects where he is Managing Director.

Mok's projects have received critical acclaim both locally and internationally. His work has been featured in numerous regional and international publications. In 2006, he was invited to exhibit at the prestigious Aedes Gallery, Berlin. In 2012, he was invited to lecture and exhibit in Milan during the Milan Furniture Fair.

Mok is an active participant on the arts scene in Singapore. He was a board member of The Substation, an alternative arts group, from 1995 to 2004. In 1996, he was awarded the Japan Chamber of Commerce and Industry's Singapore Foundation Arts Award. In 2010, he was

appointed by Singapore's Ministry of Information, Communications and the Arts to be a member of the Arts and Culture Strategic Review Committee. The committee was tasked with planning Singapore's next phase of cultural development until 2025.

Mok has been a part-time tutor at the Department of Architecture, National University of Singapore since 1992 and a member of the Advisory Committee for the Temasek Polytechnic School of Design from 1999 to 2003. He is also a member of various scholarship committees. He was a committee member of the Singapore Heritage Society from 1995 to 2001, and since 1996 has been a Board Member of the Urban Redevelopment Authority, Singapore's national land-use planning agency. In 1999, he was appointed as a member of Singapore's Preservation of Monuments Board and is currently serving as its Deputy Chairman.

In recognition of his contributions to Singapore's architectural scene, he was received the President's Design Award in 2007, the nation's highest honour for design.

Mok has a deep understanding of local heritage and Chinese tradition. This is apparent in all his work, expressed through the prism of a thoroughly modern sensibility. This is nowhere more evident than in his award-winning additions to the Singapore National Museum.

W ARCHITECTS
Mok Wei Wei,
Block 205, Henderson Road #04-01, Singapore 179033
(65) 6235 3113
office@w-architects.com.sg

SELECT BIBLIOGRAPHY

WOOI ARCHITECT

Wooi Lok Kuang is a corporate member of PAM (the Malaysian Institute of Architects) and a practising architect based in Kuala Lumpur, Malaysia. He is the principal of Wooi Architect, which he established at the end of November 1996. He was born in northern Malaysia where he spent his childhood among traditional Malay Villages. The authentic and sustainable way of life in the villages has greatly influenced his outlook in architecture.

Wooi spent ten years in Sydney, Australia, and obtained a Bachelor of Architecture in 1989 and subsequently a Master of Architecture in 1990 from the University of New South Wales. He is frequently invited to local universities and colleges as a guest lecturer and critic. Currently, he is Adjunct Professor to University Putra Malaysia. His designs have been recognized by PAM for excellence in architecture. He was Gold Medalist at the 2012 Architects Regional Council of Asia for the Ting Residence. His work has been extensively published both in books and in magazines.

WOOI ARCHITECT
Wooi Lok Kuang
45-3A, Level 3, OG Business Park,
Jalan Taman Tan Yew Lai, 58200 Kuala Lumpur, Malaysia
(60 3) 7782 5518, mobile (60) 12 2025318
info@wooiarchitect.com

Achmadi, Amanda, 'Indonesia: The Emergence of a New Architectural Consciousness of the Urban Middle Class', in Geoffrey London (ed.), *Houses for the 21st Century*, Singapore: Periplus Editions, 2004, pp. 28–35.

_____, 'The Quest for a New Tropical Architecture', in Amir Sidharta (ed.), *25 Tropical Houses in Indonesia*, Singapore: Periplus Editions, 2006, pp. 8–18.

Bunnag, Duangrit, 'Co-Evolving Heterogeneity', in Robert Powell, *The New Thai House*, Singapore, Select Publishing, 2003, pp. 10–21.

Chermayeff, Serge and Alexander, Christopher, *Community and Privacy: Toward a New Architecture of Humanism*, New York: Anchor Books, 1965.

Davison, Julian, *Black and White: The Singapore House 1898–1941*, Singapore: Talisman, 2006.

Kusno, Abidin, '(Re-)Searching Modernism: Indonesia After Decolonization', in William S. W. Lim and Jiat-Hwee Chang (eds), *Non West Modernist Past: On Architecture and Modernities*, Singapore: World Scientific, 2011, pp. 81–90.

Lim, William S. W., *Incomplete Urbanism: A Critical Urban Strategy for Emerging Economies*, Singapore: World Scientific Publishing, 2012.

Lim, William S. W. and Chang Jiat-Hwee (eds), *Non West Modernist Past: On Architecture and Modernities*, Singapore: World Scientific, 2011.

Lim, William and Tan Hock Beng, *Contemporary Vernacular: Evoking Traditions in Asian Architecture*, Singapore: Select Books, 1998.

London, Geoffrey (ed.), *Houses for the 21st Century*, Singapore: Periplus Editions, 2004.

McGillick, Paul, *25 Tropical Houses in Singapore and Malaysia*, Singapore: Periplus Editions, 2006.

Mehrotra, Rahul, 'Simultaneous Modernities: Contemporary Architecture in India', in William S. W. Lim and Jiat-Hwee Chang (eds), *Non West Modernist Past: On Architecture and Modernities*, Singapore: World Scientific, 2011, pp. 91–104.

Mumford, Lewis, *The Culture of Cities*, London: Secker and Warburg, 1938.

Powell, Robert, *The Modern Thai House: Innovative Design in Tropical Asia*, Singapore: Tuttle, 2012.

_____, *The New Indonesian House*, Singapore: Tuttle 2010.

_____, *The New Malaysian House*, Singapore: Periplus Editions, 2008.

_____, *The New Thai House*, Singapore: Select Publishing, 2003.

_____, *Singapore Houses*, Singapore: Tuttle, 2009.

Reyes, Elizabeth V., *25 Tropical Houses in the Philippines*, Singapore: Periplus Editions, 2005.

Robson, David, *Beyond Bawa: Modern Masterworks of Monsoon Asia*, London: Thames and Hudson, 2007.

Sidharta, Amir (ed.), *25 Tropical Houses in Indonesia*, Singapore: Periplus Editions, 2006.

ACKNOWLEDGEMENTS

There were many occasions when writing this book that I felt I was carrying the whole thing by myself. In fact, the book was only possible because of the help of many other people. The architects have been immensely supportive and patient during the book's gestation. On the ground, they have all been enormously hospitable and helpful and I have greatly appreciated their time and knowledge and the ideas they have shared during many a long conversation.

To all the owners who have so graciously allowed me and the photographic team to enter their homes, I would like to extend my deep gratitude. It is always a privilege to be invited into someone's home, especially when it as beautiful as all these are.

It has also been a privilege to work with Masano Kawana and his assistant, Ian Wong Teck Yen, who have been superbly professional and great travelling and working companions. In my work as an editor of architecture and design magazines, I deal with a lot of photographers, but Masano has to be the best and I am deeply grateful for the warm, intelligent and poetic images he has provided for the book.

I would like to thank Eric Oey at Periplus for giving me the opportunity to write the book, and for his ongoing support and invaluable advice. The book was different at its inception. I think it is now a much better book and Eric has helped facilitate that evolution at every stage.

Finally, I need to pay tribute to my indefatigable wife, Charmaine Zheng, who has provided enormous technical and logistical support and a critical eye when required. In many ways, she has made the book possible, especially with her moral support.

Paul McGillick, April 2013.

208

Published by Tuttle Publishing, an imprint of
Periplus Editions (HK) Ltd

www.tuttlepublishing.com

ISBN: 978-0-8048-4333-1

Distributed by

North America, Latin America & Europe
Tuttle Publishing
364 Innovation Drive
North Clarendon, VT 05759-9436 U.S.A.
Tel: 1 (802) 773-8930, Fax: 1 (802) 773-6993
info@tuttlepublishing.com
www.tuttlepublishing.com

Japan
Tuttle Publishing
Yaekari Building, 3rd Floor
5-4-12 Osaki
Shinagawa-ku
Tokyo 141-0032
Tel: (81) 3 5437-0171, Fax: (81) 3 5437-0755
sales@tuttle.co.jp
www.tuttle.co.jp

Asia Pacific
Berkeley Books Pte. Ltd.
61 Tai Seng Avenue, #02-12
Singapore 534167
Tel: (65) 6280-1330, Fax: (65) 6280-6290
inquiries@periplus.com.sg
www.periplus.com

15 14 13
10 9 8 7 6 5 4 3 2 1

Printed in Singapore   1306CP

The Tuttle Story: "Books to Span the East and West"

Most people are surprised to learn that the world's largest publisher of books on Asia had its humble beginnings in the tiny American state of Vermont. The company's founder, Charles Tuttle, came from a New England family steeped in publishing, and his first love was books—especially old and rare editions.

Tuttle's father was a noted antiquarian dealer in Rutland, Vermont. Young Charles honed his knowledge of the trade working in the family bookstore, and later in the rare books section of Columbia University Library. His passion for beautiful books—old and new—never wavered throughout his long career as a bookseller and publisher.

After graduating from Harvard, Tuttle enlisted in the military and in 1945 was sent to Tokyo to work on General Douglas MacArthur's staff. He was tasked with helping to revive the Japanese publishing industry, which had been utterly devastated by the war. When his tour of duty was completed, he left the military, married a talented and beautiful singer, Reiko Chiba, and in 1948 began several successful business ventures.

To his astonishment, Tuttle discovered that postwar Tokyo was actually a book-lover's paradise. He befriended dealers in the Kanda district and began supplying rare Japanese editions to American libraries. He also imported American books to sell to the thousands of GIs stationed in Japan. By 1949, Tuttle's business was thriving, and he opened Tokyo's very first English-language bookstore in the Takashimaya Department Store in Ginza, to great success. Two years later, he began publishing books to fulfill the growing interest of foreigners in all things Asian.

Though a westerner, Tuttle was hugely instrumental in bringing a knowledge of Japan and Asia to a world hungry for information about the East. By the time of his death in 1993, he had published over 6,000 books on Asian culture, history and art—a legacy honored by Emperor Hirohito in 1983 with the "Order of the Sacred Treasure," the highest honor Japan bestows upon non-Japanese.

The Tuttle company today maintains an active backlist of some 1,500 titles, many of which have been continuously in print since the 1950s and 1960s—a great testament to Charles Tuttle's skill as a publisher. More than 60 years after its founding, Tuttle Publishing is more active today than at any time in its history, still inspired by Charles Tuttle's core mission—to publish fine books to span the East and West and provide a greater understanding of each.